A powerful book which unpacks the co
maintaining a healthy and productive
today's strategies don't work. They pu
thinking focused on prevention that is pre
and effective. An essential read for anyon⸱ ᵢₙ ₐ leadership role.
  – *Karen Meager, organisational psychologist and author*

This is a great book and very aptly timed. Anyone with people
management or performance responsibilities would benefit from
reading this. Creating a more open culture, eradicating the taboo
around mental health, is the last untapped source of contribution
and capacity. A brilliant read.
  – *Deanne Perry, schools' cluster HR manager*

A thoughtful and insightful book for our times. *BRAVE New Leader*
equips current or aspiring leaders with evidence and practical,
attainable actions to be a brave, trusted, performance-driven
leader. Any leader who aims to look beneath the surface to explore
the riches of their colleagues with openness, curiosity and purpose
should harness these words to enable them to flourish and grow
with the enclosed guidance on building healthy performance
behaviours.
  – *Marcus Hunt, head of employee health and wellbeing*
  (APAC and EMEA) at a global pharmaceuticals company

An invaluable guide for leaders seeking to unlock the true potential
of their teams. This insightful book offers a comprehensive
understanding of employees' needs, motivations and aspirations,
balanced against the demands of the modern-day workplace. With
practical strategies and real-world examples, it equips the reader
with the tools to foster a positive and productive work environment.
A must-read for any BRAVE leader aiming to build strong, cohesive
teams and drive organisational success.
  – *Claire Walsh, safety and injury prevention professional*

This is a necessary book for current times. If you're a people manager or responsible for the performance and wellbeing of a team, you need to read this. Creating a culture where your team feels that their individual purpose is supported and where they have the energy for the people and things that matter most to them is no longer a nice-to-have; it's now a must-have in today's business world.

– Jason Morgan, global health and wellbeing leader

BRAVE New Leader is an inspiring and transformational read. The book challenges conventional norms and offers new insights on how to lead in the new world of work with insight, integrity, purpose and resilience. Through examples and practical advice it empowers leaders to embrace their unique strengths, foster collaboration and create a positive impact. The insights and practical advice shared are useful for any level of leader. A must for anyone aspiring to be an impactful and informed leader in a rapidly changing work environment. The book would be ideal to give to your leadership teams as it will encourage leaders to embrace change and improve decision making and collaboration. The book will have a lasting impact on teams and the whole organisation.

– Jayne Long, HR specialist and consultant

BRAVE New Leader

BRAVE
NEW LEADER

How to transform
workplace
pressure into
sustainable
performance
and growth

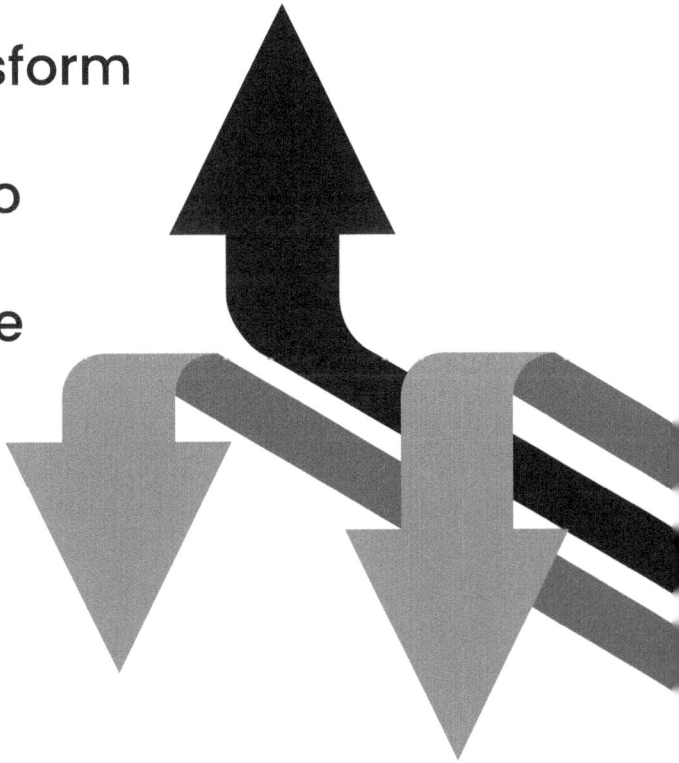

VICKY SMITH & LESLEY COOPER

BRAVE New Leader
ISBN 978-1-912300-68-6
eISBN 978-1-912300-69-3

Published in 2023 by Right Book Press
Printed in the UK

© Vicky Smith and Lesley Cooper 2023

The right of Vicky Smith and Lesley Cooper to be identified as the authors of this work has been asserted in accordance with the Copyright, Designs and Patents Act 1988.

A CIP record of this book is available from the British Library.

Contents

Introduction

Something has gone a little wrong with how we're living and working. Despite growing leadership interest in taking a more strategic approach to employee wellbeing and performance and the rapid expansion of the wellbeing industry it has fuelled, cases of workplace stress and burnout continue to rise. Sadly this suggests that the investment is missing its target. This is a problem, and not just for the people who form those statistics, whose demands and challenges have exceeded their ability to cope. Despite the radical changes that have been made to the way we work post Covid-19 pandemic, those same *human* resources are still the income generators for their companies. The stress and burnout statistics will represent only the proportion of staff who have reached the point of overwhelm. They take no account of the even greater numbers of staff who are not yet at that point. Relentless pressure to do more with the same or less is undermining the ability of many employees to perform at their best, or even at all.

An employee sustainability crisis is brewing which the proliferation of wellbeing support and resilience development programmes seem unable to address. This is not surprising to us because most of what's on offer in the wellbeing space – most notably counselling and therapeutic services as well as help with building resiliency – does nothing to understand or address the source of all that pressure and the problems it causes. These offerings alleviate the symptoms or provide short-term protection from the stressors themselves but at best they are like sticking plasters on broken windows (see Chapter 4).

Employer and employee workplace expectations are rapidly changing. Companies need accountability, commitment, full engagement and 'always on' contribution. Employees now want more from their jobs, especially valuing greater levels of flexibility when offered. Yet they're also fatigued by the constant conflict between the needs of the business and their personal needs, purpose and responsibilities.

Intellectual capital is still the king of competitive advantage and, as a result, leaders are under even more pressure to attract and retain key talent from a global workforce. But many employees are voting with their feet, no longer willing to accept excessively long working hours and inexorable pressure. Part of the sustainability problem is a kind of collective myopia among senior leadership about what the employee experience might be. This may be due to a lack of interest in the topic, a lack of time to investigate it or fear of what might emerge if they open Pandora's box. It's likely to be a mix of all three.

Let's not forget that leaders are people too and they face their own sustainability challenges. They're often ground down by a challenging economic climate and unrelenting pressure to deliver better results year on year with the same or even fewer resources. This leads to shortcuts, a short-term mindset and pressure pushed further down the organisation to a workforce who are, in many cases, already operating at maximum capacity and feeling the strain. It's hardly surprising therefore that many of their staff are being fast-tracked to chronic stress and overwhelm.

This situation is compounded by the fact that many organisations are so psychologically unsafe that people who are struggling find it difficult to tell anyone or to have the autonomy or ability to directly adjust their work demands. Few employees feel brave enough to put forward their ideas, try new approaches that might help them or simply say they need a little downtime to recover. They believe (often correctly) that their workplace isn't ready to hear it. So they soldier on, trying to work smarter or faster or both, until their performance nosedives and their wellbeing is compromised. This accounts for the popularity of company-funded counselling services.

Pressure will continue to be a pervasive presence in modern life and work – and pressure isn't necessarily a bad thing. However, to create an environment that's conducive to employees being able to manage their pressure in the ways that work for them, and to speak up when demands exceed their ability to cope, leaders must role model behaviours that *support,* rather than undermine, employee sustainability. They also need to create the conditions that encourage and allow employees to effectively manage their personal energy resources and in so doing build their resilience and capacity. This generates a true win–win. Employees stay accountable, committed and happily engaged without burning out in the process. To achieve this, what's needed is an improvement in workplace psychological safety.

In the 25-plus years that we've been practising as wellbeing and performance consultants, we've gained first-hand knowledge of the fallout from all the performance-depleting corporate behaviours talked about in this book, which is what prompted us to write it. Just like the people we support, we too have experienced pushback while operating inside companies that could have been psychologically safer. Despite our positive intentions, we've lost goodwill while leaders stirred up fear and stifled the creativity we were engaged to bring to the table.

More open and human collaborations are of benefit to everyone as they allow the best possible return on the time and energy invested. Despite everyone's best efforts to do so, time can't be expanded – it truly is the most democratic of resources. Therefore the best way forward in our 'do more with less', volatile, uncertain, complex and ambiguous world is to cultivate openness, be able to tell it like it is, try new approaches and fail faster if it doesn't work. Nobody has all the answers and everyone can learn from the experience of others.

Now more than ever, employees need to operate inside a workplace envelope that encourages bravery – to be able to stick their head above the parapet, share what they know and do the right thing, if it's the right thing to do. Acting with authenticity and integrity requires a level of confidence and self-belief, as employees' resolve can disappear under pressure to comply with the wishes from above. What's required is a willingness to dig deep, ask difficult questions of yourself and be clear about your values and beliefs.

For employers to get the best from their human assets, they need to make it possible for them to behave in accordance with what's important to them, not just what's important to their organisations. The zero-sum game being played at present, where staff believe the only way to meet the demands placed on them is to extend the working day into what ought to be recovery time, is not sustainable. The result is clearly visible in the increased stress and burnout statistics. It becomes obvious, then, that it's dangerous to play the work game this way as it ends in a long, slow sleepwalk into disengagement and reduced wellbeing.

Wherever you are in your company hierarchy, we hope this book is a call to arms. It will help you rebuild your energy and resilience and end your silent (and likely grumbling or frustrated) compliance with the established way of doing things. We offer a pathway along which you can develop the ability to do the right thing – for you, your team and your organisation – helping you do your bit to address stress and burnout in your workplace. It will help you to step into your brave, authentic self and be the leader that others look up to, or the team member that everyone wishes they were and who inspires them with self-belief and confidence to be the change they want to see.

There will never be a better time to challenge old stories. The Covid-19 pandemic created a crack in the crust of company custom and practice. The cloud that kept everyone in the dark, repeating old ways of working and behaving, has been lifted and a new path has now been illuminated. Culture change from a cold start is slow and tough. However, the momentum is already there – employees and employers are now ready, having been forced by circumstance to invent and adopt ways of working previously considered unworkable. Where there's a commercial imperative there's often a way. As one of our clients said just three months into the global pandemic, 'It [the pandemic] has achieved in 10 weeks what would otherwise have taken 10 years in our organisation.' Recent experience shows that when necessary, meaningful change can happen really quickly. We're currently in that sweet spot where the confidence to do things differently is high, employee demands are changing and there's genuine interest and desire to explore more ethical ways of being successful. Don't let that opportunity slip away. In this book we will show you, step by step, our BRAVE methodology, helping you take action now.

❦**1** Work – a complex companion

The workplace, traditionally defined as a location external to our normal living environment, is where most people used to spend around half of their waking hours. Although the Covid-19 pandemic changed where work was done for many people, the fundamental role work played in people's lives (unless they were furloughed) stayed the same or in some cases expanded. Without the necessity to physically change location to get to work, time that was previously allocated to the commute was suddenly and delightfully liberated. Initially this bonus time was reappropriated away from work – the number of people seen pounding the pavement in trainers or walking dogs being clear testament to this new-found freedom. However, not all that long after the initial liberation, footpaths and parks were relatively empty again and family dogs found themselves returning to their more familiar exercise routines. What happened?

The answer is nuanced and influenced by many factors, among them whether you had school-age children, were personally affected by Covid-19 or had to care for someone in your family who was. The guardrails of established care networks and day to day routines that shaped and supported pre-pandemic life buckled in the heat of the crisis. Almost overnight, everyone adapted to their new circumstances in similar yet individual ways – the impacts were specific and so was the coping response. Despite differences in the detail of the response, the speed with which people adapted their behaviour was universal. If companies were able to keep paying their staff, and in some cases even if they could not, and however difficult it became with elder care, home schooling or separation from colleagues and resources, employees found a way to keep working. Work–life boundaries blurred, personal anxiety increased and complexities mounted as the pandemic wore on. But individuals and teams paddled relentlessly in turbulent waters, doing all they could to keep the boat the right way up and do their bit to meet company objectives, whatever the personal difficulty.

The significant place that engagement with work, loyalty to colleagues and bosses, fear of failure and the yearning for success occupies in employees' psyches was never easier to observe than during the pandemic. Workers couldn't be with each other physically but the rapid escalation of digital connectivity removed the barrier to keeping the company boat moving forward. A 2020 study conducted by Harvard Business School strategy unit analysing the digital activity of 3,143,270 people in Europe, North America and the Middle East found that the number of meetings people attended increased by 12.9 per cent and the number of attendees per meeting increased by 13.5 per cent. However, the average length of meetings decreased (down 20.1 per cent). Collectively, although the net effect was that people spent less time in meetings than they had pre-lockdown (down 11.5 per cent), there were 'significant and durable increases in the length of the average workday' (8.2 per cent, increasing by more than 48.5 minutes). Across the globe, employees worked longer hours and made more connections than they did before, making sure the show carried on.

Work is where the most significant proportion of waking time, energy and, particularly for knowledge workers, cerebral attention is invested. Daily contact with colleagues and superiors historically meant that the workplace was the arena for forging enduring relationships and laying the foundations for long-lasting careers and affiliations. The impact that work has on the shape of a life greatly exceeds the sum of the tasks involved. Responding to the demands and challenges of work and the juggling act that often ensues from aligning these pressures with other roles and responsibilities dominates employee thinking time. But this isn't necessarily a bad thing. Studies (eg Waddell & Burton 2006) continue to show that fulfilling job roles can have a dramatic impact on a person's overall psychological wellbeing, both at work and in their personal life. Good work is good for you. The reverse is also true, of course – working in a disharmonious or consistently highly pressurised environment can have an equally detrimental effect on employee welfare. So what is it about work that means it so easily dominates and remains the top priority, even in the face of multiple other equally legitimate claims on time and attention? What does it offer (apart from money) and why exactly is 'good work' so beneficial and rewarding?

Why work?

Most people's instinctive response to the 'why work?' question is that they do it for the money – a necessary activity to generate the income to fund a life. These economic fundamentals are undoubtedly a factor. However, the fervour with which employees have responded in the past decade to the rapid acceleration and accumulation of work demands suggests that, up until the pandemic at least, this is not all there is to it. Previous generations had a more noticeable culture of working to live – liking your job was a bonus but regardless of your feelings, it was primarily a means to an end. Nowadays, employees expect more from the work transaction – as evidenced by the number of people who changed jobs immediately after the pandemic, during what Anthony Klotz, professor of management at University College London's School of Management, referred to in May 2021 as 'the Great Resignation'. During this period common reasons for leaving jobs included low pay, limited or non-existent opportunities for career advancement or simply feeling disrespected. The labour force is shrinking and as a result, despite economic uncertainties, workers are more mobile than ever before – keen to find roles that not only pay the bills but also offer intellectual interest and flexibility.

In the modern, multi-generational workforce, different age groups seek similar things but in varying proportions depending on their life stage. Young people who are starting out in their careers and are as yet unencumbered by children or mortgage commitments tend to be focused on self-development, career enhancement and building useful social networks. Once family commitments become a factor, the focus can shift to the desire for meaningful work, delivered to maximum efficiency in order to balance the demands of work and life. For a more seasoned employee, the focus can shift again to feeling able to share knowledge and experience and contribute in a lasting way to the organisation's intellectual capital. Whatever the specific needs, people now expect more from work than they once did. In return they're clearly prepared to invest a lot of themselves into it in order to extract what they desire from it. Far from work being just the means to another (higher purpose) end, succeeding at work has become the end in itself.

Recognising this shift is central to understanding the relationship between work, employee wellbeing and performance. A contributor to *TIME* magazine commented in May 2021 that since the pandemic, 'We have been living at work.' (Lipman 2021) Although this comment was specifically referring to the effect of 'obliterated' boundaries between work and life as a consequence of home working, it serves as a moniker for the modern approach to work more generally. Succeeding at work invariably means meeting or exceeding some form of targeted contribution to the company objectives and for many doing so has become the higher purpose, independently of the opportunity costs involved.

Many of the drivers of this shift are rooted in the shape of the pre-Covid workplace. What until that time was still thought of as the 'modern' way of working was not, in practical terms, very modern at all. It was based on a post-Second World War military model of clear and familiar hierarchies for men, a nine to five working day and the near absence of childcare responsibilities. As any working parent of either sex knows, this underlying model has obvious and serious flaws. Yet despite universal acknowledgement of the shortcomings, more than a faint outline of the original blueprint persisted. As a result, many people working inside this envelope have been trying to meet the demands of present-day life while operating within a system that's anything but congruent.

The inevitable result has been the repeated – but, important to note, not necessarily unwilling – erosion of observable boundaries between work and life. The blurring of boundaries was under way well before the pandemic, having started as soon as mobile communication devices were in every coat pocket, but lockdown threw the drift into sharp relief.

What lies behind this willingness to repurpose time once reserved for family, friends and personal pursuits? Why do so many people feel compelled to divert time away from the activities, interests and relationships that form the foundation of who they are *as a person*? We find ourselves saying quite regularly that when we employ someone the whole person comes to work, not just the bit that does the job. This is objectively true (and is a theme that will be developed fully as this book progresses) but there's undoubtedly a powerful force at work, one that prompts what people 'do' at work to shape how they organise their life and apportion the rest of their time. Human motivation is a complex area of psychology and too large to dive into in detail here. However, two generalised fundamentals will shine a little light onto our species' increasingly close and complicated association with the workplace.

The first of these is that humans are hard wired to make cognitive connections and look for meaning in all things. The second, and it's highly correlated with the first, is that humans are also natural and inveterate storytellers. It's the ability to build 'internal stories' about things that enables us to establish connections and find meaning in the most disparate or apparently inert situations. This extends naturally to the workplace. *Homo sapiens*' storytelling skills are baked in. Our brain circuitry evolved to shuffle, select and process the mission critical (for which read physical survival) from the myriad of environmental data that floods in, via the senses, from the outside world. A series of important filters – which we will cover shortly – order and assemble what's deemed relevant and useful so that it can be acted upon. The resulting 'internal stories' can be positive and helpful or negative and unhelpful – and usually they're a bit of both. Regardless of the resulting plot line, these narratives are constant and shape everything people see in a situation, what they feel about it and what they subsequently do. This shuffling and processing of external stimuli is so seamless (and effortless) that we're usually unaware that it's going on at all. This being the case, it should be fairly easy to see the potential implications for shaping our attitude and behaviour towards work.

As Will Storr states in the introduction to his book *The Science of Storytelling* (2019), 'We know how this ends. You're going to die and so will everyone you love. And then there will be heat death. All the change in the universe will cease, the stars will die and there'll be nothing left of anything but an infinite, dead, freezing void. Human life, in all its noise and hubris, will be rendered meaningless for all eternity.' Yet, as Storr goes on to say, looking at the energy and purpose with which most humans go about their daily lives, you could be forgiven for thinking we're ignorant of the fact. We busily spend our minutes, hours and days, he says, with the knowledge of this void hanging over us and he suggests that the 'cure' humans have created to 'hold this horror at bay' is story. Brains create stories to distract their hosts from this terrible truth and in so doing enable us to fill our lives with hopeful goals.

Not everyone will agree with his assertion of course, as it's an uncomfortable and somewhat sobering thought. But nevertheless, the influence that this subconscious storybook has on our behaviour cannot be overestimated. It shapes what people see during their waking hours and triggers the emotions (both positive and negative) that go on to influence choices and actions. It sculpts the quality of connection between friends, colleagues and family members, defining how much information people feel comfortable sharing about themselves or what they know. It's impossible to live and work without stories – they fill television screens and cinemas, newspapers and journals, online games and pastimes, blogs and podcasts, newsfeeds, social media activities – in fact every interaction with every other human. They're even present when we're asleep, in the form of dreams.

Our stories make us who we are and we subconsciously construct them about everything. In every household, workplace, classroom, bar, club, restaurant or place of worship – indeed anywhere that humans gather – there will be a cognitive library full of private narratives, each one unique to the brain that's spooling it. We navigate our way through life using stories as a reference point for deciding what's important (or not), why this or that just happened and, most importantly, what's probably going to happen next (or so we think!). Just how reliable these stories are is rarely considered, of course, and that's why we're interested in them in this book – but we mustn't get ahead of ourselves.

Awareness of how our storytelling brains 'inform' us of what's going on in the world is central to understanding the modern relationship with work. Everybody at work has multiple internal stories running about their current job, the people they work with and why they're doing it. These narratives will have a cast of many, alongside a plethora of personal hopes, goals, ambitions, fears, preoccupations, strongly held values, attributed meanings and beliefs – all nested inside each other like Russian dolls. In the same way that DNA holds instructions for cells to combine in ways that will enable specific functions, internal stories shape and direct the way people interact with each other. Despite their huge influence, stories run unconsciously and are therefore rarely challenged. This matters in this context because what you tell yourself about your work and the people you work with has a huge bearing on how you go about doing the work.

These compelling internal narratives are the reason why so many people willingly trade 'off work' time for 'more work' time, extending the working day to get more done. They create a mille-feuille of unarticulated beliefs, layered with anxieties about the possible negative consequences of this or that not being achieved on time or a target missed. The internal narrative of 'keep going until it's done' becomes increasingly louder, drowning out other options. The fear of an outcome more uncomfortable than the disruption of other plans repeatedly drives the decision to prioritise the work task over other scheduled activities.

This fearful narrative will normally feature at least one 'must' and several 'becauses', but often these lines of thought don't have an articulated end, just a feeling that the consequences of not achieving the objective will probably erase the benefits of doing what might have been planned for that time. Previous experience may mean there's no need to complete the thought as you've already 'read the book'. In effect these narratives equate to flipping through the first few chapters until you have enough 'data' to anticipate what happens at the end. All you know is that non-delivery is likely to attract criticism so you'd best keep on going.

As stated earlier, humans are also highly purposeful, as well as great storytellers. These two defining characteristics are inextricably linked. In the huge sweep of the universe, it could be argued that what we do on our planet is pretty insignificant. But as Storr points out, to see us going about our daily business you wouldn't think so – our existence has significance for us. Humans care deeply about many, many things – people, places, memories, plans, failures, reputation, the future, the past. Everything means something precisely because we're hard wired to look for meanings and bundle them into something to respond to.

People have what psychologist Viktor Frankl refers to in his book *Man's Search for Meaning* as 'the will to meaning' (1985). We're programmed to look for meaning in all things and when we find it, it propels us forward. It becomes our personal mission and purpose. A few people can describe their personal purpose specifically – being precise about what they believe, why they believe it and what they want to achieve with their life. They can sometimes even tell you whether their day to day behaviour is taking them towards or away from their private and professional goals. Many others find it harder to articulate their purpose, often falling back on a vague sense of what they value or what 'feels or looks right' to them. The ability to be precise about purpose isn't related to its influence – you don't have to be able to describe the chemical composition of air to breathe it. Whether or not it's clearly stated, purpose propels people through life.

Like so much about us as a species, there's an evolutionary basis to this deep need for meaning and it's related to a corresponding need for and acceptance by others. In order to feel safe we need to feel as if we belong. Our ancestors were hunter-gatherers but this way of life was replaced by cooperation in groups. Being alert to subtle physical or behavioural signals and being able to 'catch the mood' and join in became a survival advantage. Not surprisingly, people still have this ability to detect the prevailing wind within their 'band' and adjust their sails accordingly. In short we're both comforted and excited by inclusion and feel drawn to certain situations, people and stories that inspire us, causing us to look to something bigger, better or broader than ourselves. Living conditions have changed dramatically but humans' skills for reading one another are as sharp as ever – we quickly pick up on and buy into the stories we feel we can believe in and be a part of.

This is the basis of Simon Sinek's assertion in his book *Start with Why* (2009) that 'People don't buy what you do – they buy why you do it.' Sensing purpose in another person or group of people is extremely beguiling – the more meaningful it is, often the more we want to relate to it. In *The Culture Code* (2018), Daniel Coyle cites a story of a US entrepreneur who intentionally avoids introductory meetings, tours and schedules when recruiting. Instead, he sets up orientation opportunities with a simple mailout giving the address of the site and a note reading 'Meet these people. Then ask them who else you should meet.' One candidate (who, like many others before her, actually moved state to join the project) reported, 'It was like I was getting this signal that got stronger with everyone I talked to... and I couldn't resist. I ended up moving here. It wasn't logical at all. It was like I had to do it.' Connecting to a mission is a bit like getting the whiff of a pheromone.

The performance benefits of tapping into employees' (and customers') love of belonging is well understood by the world's corporations, many of which have devised specific purpose statements to aid employee and customer engagement. Some have gone further and now describe themselves as 'purpose-driven' organisations, detailing their higher purpose ideals and ambitions to encourage employees to consciously connect to them. A few organisations have done this exceptionally well, ensuring such close alignment with these statements that they can justifiably claim that what they do and how they do it acts as the necessary proof of why they do it. This is the gold standard version of being purpose-driven.

Many others are riding the purpose wave but alignment of the day to day is not always as tight as it could be. Strategy is set and communicated, often beautifully wrapped in a carefully crafted corporate purpose statement. Employees are urged to define their personal mission and connect it to the corporate one, aligning what they want for themselves with the purpose goals of their employer. This approach works because, as these companies know, the energy, engagement and contribution boost of connecting personal purpose to corporate mission is akin to coming off battery power and switching to the mains. The 'taking people with us' strategy is much more effective than the artfully photographed motivational whale tails that once proudly adorned boardroom walls.

The zero-sum problem

So far, so sensible; in terms of job and organisational satisfaction as well as employee wellbeing and performance, the rewards are logically going to be there when all the narratives align. There is, however, an inconvenient problem. The model completely overlooks the real possibility that the two purposes – personal and corporate – might on occasion be mutually exclusive. Taking consistent and tidy alignment of the two missions as a given ignores the much more likely reality that while there are huge benefits in alignment, on a practical level they may be at odds with each other. Life events may regularly confound the plan and achieving one may only be possible at the expense of the other. What happens when these come into conflict? How do you resolve a situation where pursuing one purpose leads to the compromise or abandonment of the other? What happens when boundaries between the two become so blurred they're nearly impossible to see – when you're emotionally, if not practically, 'living at work'? Far from greasing the wheels of engagement and performance, the conflict leaves employees to find ways to practise damage limitation on the fallout resulting from a grinding misalignment and painfully divided loyalties.

The inner life of employees is shaped by personal purpose, including goals they've set for themselves, which will probably feature some professional or career development targets. Nestled inside that personal purpose will be an array of aspirations, attitudes and values related to topics as varied as parenting, care for a partner and wider family, perhaps their spiritual life or other intellectual, sporting and social pursuits – the gamut of human experience. These day to day preoccupations shape a person but are often supplemented with the twin drive to belong and make a meaningful contribution. The mission and purpose of our employer often meets this need and employees are drawn to this too. As we said before, when you employ someone the whole person comes to work – not just the part that does the job. People bring all their other preoccupations and attributes with them too, many of which are equally if not more valuable than the specific skills you hired them for. When people are unable to balance the demands of work with the rest of their lives – when they're forced to consistently prioritise work over other activities – the time to do the extra work is inevitably diverted away from the activities that align with their personal purpose. When that happens they lose something intensely valuable both to themselves and their employer. Progress towards or alignment with personal purpose grounds and anchors people but like everything worth having, achieving that requires investment. When the funds of time are diverted, people become vulnerable to life's storms. Private connections that stabilise, renew and bolster strength are eroded and when life's ill winds blow, anchorage is compromised.

Big trees and taproots

To bring this point to life in our own work, we often ask people to consider how likely it is that a broadleaf tree with a full canopy but only a taproot instead of a spreading root system would still be upright after a gale. It's possible to estimate the spread of a tree's root system by taking a look at the canopy – they will be roughly the same. Nature sees to it that the more extensive the canopy, the wider the spread of roots and connections to nourish and secure the tree.

However, as our roles and responsibilities expand through life – as our metaphorical canopy grows – meeting all those demands requires us to regularly divert time away from the very activities that ground and secure us. When this becomes the regular response strategy to frequent work–life conflict, a personal wellbeing and sustainability problem will be on the cards.

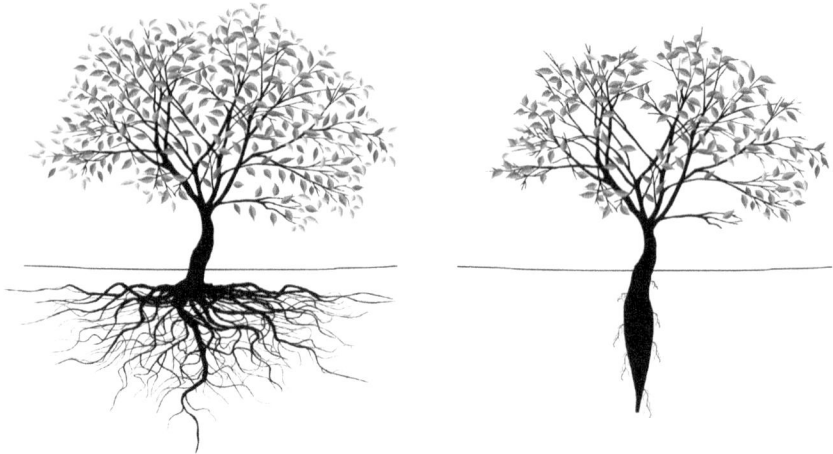

Figure 1: The importance of anchorage

Despite knowing this intuitively, when it comes down to it, work invariably wins out. Nearly 60 per cent of people using our pressure and resilience assessment tools either very strongly agree or strongly agree with the statement 'If I feel under pressure at work I tend to stop making time for exercise or social activities'. The conflict between personal and corporate is usually resolved by prioritising work over non-work – the non-work Peter is robbed to pay the workload Paul.

The net result of these divided or conflicting loyalties is clearly visible in the stress and burnout headlines we see every day. The UK Health and Safety Executive estimates that more than half of all workplace ill health episodes have stress as a causal factor and one in six employees have a diagnosable mental health impairment (2022). Little wonder then that engagement with tertiary emotional support services such as employee assistance programmes, mental health first aid and counselling is so high. The way employers are currently navigating these conflicting drives is certainly not working for employees and their families and for this reason it won't be working all that well for companies either.

As we mentioned earlier, the significant labour movements that followed the pandemic suggest that many employees seized a moment to resolve this conflict in a decisive way. The demolition of work–life boundaries during lockdown, coupled with the lived experience of operating inside a radically different model for work, prompted many employees to review the alignment of their time and energy with their personal mission and purpose. Those choosing to prioritise their own and their families' needs left their jobs in droves.

McKinsey (2022) refers to this behaviour as 'the Great Attrition', which saw more than 4.3 million US workers voluntarily leave their jobs in December 2021, only slightly below a record high figure the month before. Those leaving took very different roles or in some cases left the workforce entirely. Post pandemic it's clear that people are looking for more control of their work lives and more opportunity to set their own schedules and protect personal boundaries. According to McKinsey, midlifers say they're 'looking for more emotionally sustainable and rewarding working conditions' and employees now crave 'investment in the human aspects of work' and want 'a renewed and revised sense of purpose' – one that presumably aligns more often than it clashes with their own. They want social and interpersonal connections with their colleagues and managers and to feel a sense of shared identity – meaningful interactions, not just transactions. The employee's why is gaining ground on the company's.

This is potentially great news, as aligning purpose in this way leads to better mental health, increased engagement and performance and improved job and organisational satisfaction. However, there's much work to be done before these benefits are fully realised. In fact, the statistics on stress and mental health at work tell us that the direction of travel is going the wrong way. For example, the number of new and longstanding cases of stress and anxiety has risen by 14 per cent since 2020/2021 (Health & Safety Executive 2022). Many thousands of employees challenged and updated some old stories about what's possible but unfortunately far fewer of the companies they work for did the same.

Knowing your personal why

So what's your story? Why do you approach work the way you do? What personal purpose is attached to it? What rationalisations do you give yourself (and others) for how you divide your energy and attention between work and other aspects of your life? Do you feel you're getting the balance right? If you've never really considered these questions, you're not alone. Modern life is so speedy now there's little time to ponder what you do or why you do it. As habit-driven beings who generally feel most comfortable when things are stable and predictable, humans are hard wired for this tendency. When the pressure is on – and it seemingly always is – people will tend to default to doing what they normally do (but often attempt to do it faster), drawing on the belief that it has worked until now so it's probably sensible to keep doing it.

However, these questions are posed for good reason. Getting a firmer, more honest grasp on your personal why and being able to describe to yourself what you find meaningful at work is a prerequisite both for protecting mental wellbeing and unlocking full performance potential. Intentionally reflecting on the extent to which what you do every day aligns with your inner purpose is a vital first step towards achieving personal sustainability. The pace, uncertainty and complexity of modern life are increasing rapidly. If you want to stay on top, subtle recalibrations in the way you respond to these external pressures will be necessary. When *what* you do every day illustrates *why* you do it, you not only avoid stressful and exhausting personal conflict but others are often inspired to follow suit. When these things are not aligned, you're effectively flying with crossed controls, which is not only wasteful of energy but even more importantly sends the wrong messages to others about what really matters to you.

If you want to live it, a clear line of sight on your personal purpose is obviously important. Just as importantly, heightened awareness of what you're telling yourself in any situation can help you remember that your individual stories are likely to differ from other people's. The aforementioned tendency to repeat specific and preferred behaviours, combined with the accelerating pace of life, means you can erroneously assume that the absence of pushback means that everyone has bought into what you're trying to achieve and is comfortable with the steps you're taking to get there. Because you're excited about an opportunity and can visualise the benefits in glorious technicolour, it usually suits you to believe that everyone else can see the same things in the same way. But, as we said before, it's not just the skillset that turns up for work each day – specific, task-focused capabilities are accompanied by a human with unique lived experience, biases, blind spots, anxieties and fears as well as hopes and joys. In other words, internal stories come to work too and people are as wedded to theirs as you are to yours. There are therefore multiple dangers in riding roughshod over them.

An ear for a whispered story – the interpersonal advantage

Whatever place you currently occupy in your organisation's hierarchy, getting the best from yourself and others (and helping all parties to stay well in the process) means sharpening up your hearing in relation to both your own stories and those of others. If you accept that outlooks and perspectives differ and are actively curious about what form those differences might take, you'll have much more productive collaborations at all levels. Lack of interest or concern in someone else's outlook, much like stroking a dog's coat against the lie of the fur, generates a negative charge and discomfort for both parties. By contrast, awareness of and active engagement with the perspectives of others is akin to stroking the coat in the direction that the fur lies, producing an outcome that's more comfortable and productive for both parties.

Whenever fixed or limited resources are combined with an imperative for economic growth, the response will inevitably be to look for ways of doing more with the same or less. It's quite likely that this characterises your workplace. You may recognise other challenges being talked about, such as:

- ★ how to manage inclusion inside a workforce that's more diverse in age and ethnicity
- ★ how to respond to a labour market that's both shrinking and ageing
- ★ how to recruit and retain talent now that the people you want to hire and keep are more mobile and specific about what they want the company to do for them.

Then there are considerations around how to develop the right strategy for hybrid working and creating more agile models for teamwork to respond to this shift in employee expectations.

The bottom line is that all these challenges are easier to address with a more developed ear for story. When you can hear yours you can liberate yourself from stories that drive negative behaviour and prevent you from being the best version of yourself every day. Small recalibrations to these habits are often all that's required to free up disproportionately large amounts of capacity to meet the increasingly complex demands of life and work. By running the 'right' tape you can set appropriate goals and move towards them more purposefully. You can avoid wasted effort and divert unnecessary frustration and negativity. In short, you can perform better in all areas of your life. Even more significantly, you'll be a better listener. When we quieten our own stories it becomes possible to tune into those told by colleagues, friends and family, where there may be much to learn and act upon.

If you happen to be a people manager, then there's a third and specific form of storytelling for you to consider – the story you tell through the medium of your behaviour as a leader. When you were growing up you may well have heard a more senior family member (perhaps ruefully) remark 'Don't do as I do, do as I say' or, if you have children of your own, you may even have said the same thing. When managers fail to role model the behaviours that they expect from others or implement policies and procedures that are misaligned with stated or agreed values, or set targets and expectations at a level that requires employees to regularly bust boundaries to meet them, then they're telling mutually incompatible stories. The manager says one thing but the decision making and interpersonal behaviour that team members experience day to day communicate something quite different. This lack of congruence is the wellspring of workplace toxicity, stress, anxiety, fear, reduced engagement and attrition. Not surprisingly therefore our advice is to recognise the need for congruence and take responsibility for it. It's an integral part of good leadership, not an added extra. Help is provided to achieve this in later chapters of this book.

The senior leadership burden of responsibility

If you're a senior leader, the weight of responsibility for the congruence of messages is greater still. Everything that has been said up to this point obviously also applies to senior leadership. The entry requirements are a critical ear for your own and others' perspectives, curiosity about how they might differ and accepting responsibility for ensuring compatibility between corporate message and corporate behaviour. But there's a fourth critical dimension to consider. No corporate decision can ever be taken in a vacuum. Decisions made and expectations set in the boardroom, as they move from idea to implementation, inevitably and directly extend or truncate options for those working further down the company hierarchy.

If you already lead what you consider to be a purpose-driven organisation, you need to ask yourself whether your company's what – the decisions you make, how you communicate and implement those decisions and the way you organise resources – unequivocally stands as evidence of your stated why (purpose) in action. Or does it tell a different, more inconvenient story – that you don't really mean it? Are you promoting and celebrating personal mission and purpose yet at the same time asking your staff to repeatedly prioritise the company objectives over their own?

Chapter 1: Big questions

* If you're a **team member**: how good are you at hearing your own narrative, being curious about the narratives of others and tapping into them, in order to avoid conflict between opposing goals?
* If you're a **people manager**: how are you demonstrating that you're walking the talk and modelling the behaviours you seek from others?
* If you're a **senior leader**: how do you fulfil your responsibility for ensuring alignment of decision-making behaviour with the company rhetoric around vision and values?

Key messages

* Human beings are highly mission driven and are hard wired to build internal narratives about what's going on around them and what to do next. That story is shaped by their values and experiences and will inform their decision making.
* Recognising and working with the personal narratives of others fuels connection and collaborative energy. Cutting across them fuels disconnection and creates conflict and tension.
* Personal and company missions are often mutually exclusive and it's invariably left to the employee to resolve at personal, social and emotional cost to themselves. Not proactively helping employees to navigate the resulting conflict is counterproductive. Forcing an employee to consistently choose the job over other aspects of their life effectively disables their most valuable asset – the ability to do the job.

⚘2 Doing more with less

Some weeks you conquer   Some you get through   Some you merely survive

These days, there are more claims on your attention than you can possibly meet. People who are middle aged and older will remember a time when they sat on trains and looked quietly out of the window. If you're Gen Y or Z the chances are you may never have done this, born as you were into a world of mobile phones and the instant distraction they offer. Everywhere you go someone, or something, is trying to get your attention. These myriad intrusions compete hard for it – flashing or scrolling, exhorting this or that, using visual imagery or beeps, squeaks, pings and bongs. Our Stone Age brains, finely tuned over millennia to detect tiny movements, are subjected daily to sensory bombardment and information overload. The automatic luxury of snippets of downtime that used to be offered throughout the day as we sat on buses, stood in queues or just sat and ate a sandwich in the park for ten minutes has all but disappeared. Now, everybody seems to be constantly distracted by something more immediate.

As Linda Stone (2009) points out in her study of multitasking at Microsoft, we're living in a permanent state of continuous partial attention. This study is approaching 15 years old, yet in more recent years the number of claims on our mental attention has increased further. Consequently, we are, she says, everywhere but where we need to be. This has direct relevance to our ability to stay focused on the things that mean the most to us. However committed we might be towards fulfilling our objectives for this particular hour, the disruptions we're offered are relentless and distracting by design. This constant deflection from the people and tasks to which we would prefer to give our attention is doubly energy draining. Many of the people that we speak to say they frequently feel overwhelmed by the stimulus of their day and are often exhausted by the intensity of response required to keep on top of it. This is fully supported by our own data where 54 per cent of respondents agree strongly or very strongly with the statement 'I feel physically and emotionally drained at the end of the work day'. People often go on to say that despite knowing they have been fully occupied, at speed, all day/week/year they still feel they have made no headway with their objectives.

Things are often no better away from work. Working parents may have limited time with their family and you can probably picture the scene. The parents are sitting on sun loungers, one child is splashing about in the pool on her own, calling to her parents and brother to join her. Mum is on her phone responding to urgent emails and doesn't even hear her daughter. Dad gets up and puts on his flip-flops and it does look as if he's heading towards the pool but no, he turns in the opposite direction, frantically searching for a quiet space to continue his work call without his daughter's voice intruding. Their son has his headphones in, completely focused on his video game console and doesn't hear his sister calling either. She gives up trying to get their attention – she's been here before, she knows the score and knows it's pointless to keep calling them.

This sort of example is not limited to vacations. The same destructive variant of an attention crisis is playing out in workplaces. If the world outside your front door is clamorous, the world of work is similarly frenetic and if the stress statistics are to be believed,

26

potentially even more injurious. Most jobs now require workers to navigate growing demands from multiple stakeholders, simultaneously. Of course, every demand is urgent and of equal priority, at least as far as the clamouring stakeholders are concerned. This is energy draining in its own right but as we saw in the previous chapter, these demands and challenges coexist with the employee's own objectives and sense of purpose. Insert into this scenario continuous, thrumming pressure from higher-ups to deliver to the highest standard possible with fewer available resources than are probably needed. Then overlay this with personal internal concerns such as fear of negative consequences if you make a mistake. Now the stress statistics start to make a lot of sense. A whopping 67 per cent of responders to an item in our assessment tool that explores the toxic combination of high workload and tight deadlines report that they definitely or very definitely feel pressure from 'too much to do in too little time'. It certainly appears that there's too much work and too little time to do it, creating a sense of 'time famine' (Dreher 2018). Just about every team we work with, across many varied sectors, answers this question in the same way. Despite this, companies seem remarkably sanguine about it. They probably shouldn't be, as workplace pressure that's experienced this way, particularly when it results in exhaustion, usually results in disengagement. Employees who are asked to consistently do more than they feel they can with the time and resources they have eventually withdraw emotional engagement as a coping strategy. It's therefore highly likely that many people leaving their job during the Great Resignation would have been in this category. The rapid acceleration in the pace of life and work has affected people in many different ways. But running through all their adaptations and supported by all their 'enabling' (some would say disabling) technology is the narrative that to keep growing or just stay competitive they need to find ways to achieve more with the same or fewer resources.

Working with what you have

We should say straight away that for the sake of our planet, humans do need to find ways of doing the same (or better) with fewer natural resources. As far as the environmental agenda goes, there's no question that this should be our general approach. However, there are different factors at play when we think about how this might apply to our human resources. Doing more with the same or less in a manufacturing environment might mean making sure the production line runs 24 hours a day. But unlike manufacturing machines, robots, AI, other computer programs and the devices they run on, human beings are not calibrated to be always 'on'. Production can be sped up by literally moving the process along a bit faster. Capacity can be increased by adding additional machinery or, with data processing, additional RAM. But it doesn't work this way for humans. Processing output and speed cannot be increased simply by adding more storage and there are limits to how much contribution people can make before they burn out. Human performance is powered by something much more subtle and complex, yet the typical approach to wellbeing and performance sustainability suggests otherwise. There's always an upper limit on how much more output is possible, particularly if nothing else changes to facilitate the release of additional output.

The more/less quadrant model

Unlike our inorganic counterparts, thrumming away in climate-controlled server rooms, the complex organic machine that is the human being is also operating in much less stable conditions, regularly shaped and disrupted by specific internal and external factors. The pressure endemic in modern life comes from multiple internal and external sources and from various directions simul-taneously. It's felt by individuals, families, work groups and the organisations they work for. It's easy to forget, when focusing on yourself, your purpose and your work, that the company employing you is also under pressure. Each organisation faces daily pressure to stay trading and profitable. In a world dominated by global competition and expectation for growth, external performance pressure can be relentless. We illustrate the way that these pressures interrelate using this simple quadrant model.

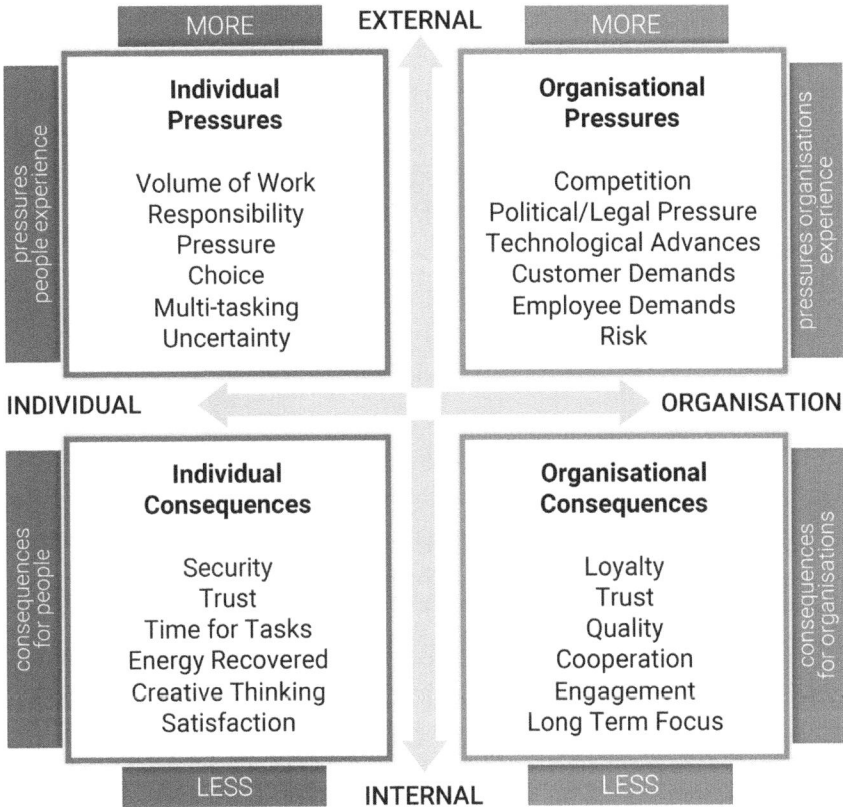

Figure 1: The more/less quadrant model (inspired by Schwartz et al 2010)

In a global economy, modern companies face much stiffer competition than they once did. To stay competitive they often respond by 'tightening the belt' – trimming staff to keep costs down and profits high. However, costs may increase in response to additional political and legal pressures as well as the need to invest in and adapt to continuously changing technology. When companies delight their customers by going the 'extra mile', that additional ground is quickly adopted as the 'expected mile', creating a relentless upward trajectory in customer expectation, often not matched by additional payments for the extra resources invested. Employees' expectations also change with each successive generation of workers, with Gen X, Y and Z all looking for subtly different conditions to stay fully engaged.

Contingent with these external organisational pressures is the deferred pressure experienced by employees living and working in this environment. Leaner workforces contain real people feeling real strain as, with previous coworkers having left, they absorb the additional workload. They're also dealing with constant uncertainty from rapidly evolving technology and shifting priorities. Keeping all these balls in the air with multiple stakeholder groups invariably leads to the type of multitasking that's emotionally and mentally draining. Constantly switching focus and attention increases the possibility that mistakes get made and worry, fear, negativity and insecurity rise. Internal pressure can build inexorably at the individual level, as each employee tries to find ways to respond to proliferating and often conflicting demands. The 'must win' narrative familiar to many (recruiters often actively select for precisely this performance mindset) fuels the private internal story that 'not doing this isn't an option', or that 'I can't let my manager down'. This way of thinking primes the personal decision-making algorithm to prioritise contribution over recovery. In doing so, it increases the risk of stress and burnout. Just as importantly, as performance stretch turns to emotional strain, the employee loses the ability to experiment or take creative risks that might lead to the discovery of more innovative or cost-effective solutions. When this happens, the cutting edge of organisational creativity and competitiveness is blunted by default; there's no bandwidth to try anything different so everyone keeps on doing the same thing but faster.

In this environment, as more and more people feel the strain, the level of workplace toxicity rises and work gratification seeps away. First observed as an increase in sickness absence, it's eventually and inevitably followed by emotional disengagement and finally resignations. Those that tend to remain are the 'still engaged but not yet cynical' and the 'more cynical than engaged' cohorts. The first cohort continues to push forward, holding it all together through sheer commitment, while the second category spreads negativity and slows everything down. Unsurprisingly, performance declines, quality drops and people become disenfranchised, creating even more risk for the organisation.

Pressure and performance

What each factor included in the model has in common, either singly or through collective effect, is to create pressure for employees. This is as good a place as any to say that pressure and stress are not the same thing, although as terms they're often conflated. There's a vital difference between the two which, with better understanding and more leadership curiosity about which factors cause one to morph into the other, can be mined to fast-track teams to more healthy and sustainable wellbeing and performance outcomes.

The difference between pressure and stress is that pressure is a neutral input – it's just there. Its sources are numerous and like atmospheric pressure at concentrations that are normal for you, you won't feel it. Stress, though, is a potential negative outcome of that pressure and therefore is not neutral. But stress is neither the only nor the inevitable outcome from pressure. There's another more positive and performance-enhancing outcome available, as pressure is the natural and helpful catalyst to personal growth and development. Without pressure to get somewhere we might never have learned to walk. Painful collisions with the floor or furniture may have been involved but the internal pressure to 'get over there' meant you risked and accomplished it. Nature sees to it that humans don't waste personal resources. We tend to use (or under-use) them until we need to raise our game. Importantly, we need that bit of necessity – that pressure – to create the personal drive we need in ourselves to face a challenge, fight a fear, master a new skill or tackle a task we feel underprepared for. As the late Rabbi Dr Abraham Twerski says in a rather wonderful YouTube video (JInsider 2009), the stimulus for a lobster to grow a new shell is that it feels itself under uncomfortable pressure in its existing one. If it didn't experience these feelings, it would never grow.

Therefore, doing more and feeling under pressure isn't the problem here. With the right conditions, feeling under pressure can be the basis of the win–win scenarios hinted at in the Introduction.

At some level, then, pressure is beneficial, as demonstrated by the Yerkes–Dodson law (Wikipedia 2004), which dictates that performance is correlated with pressure. The law states that personal performance increases with physiological or mental arousal *but only up to a point*. When levels of arousal become too high, personal performance decreases, particularly in relation to more complex tasks. This process is often illustrated as a bell-shaped curve (Figure 2).

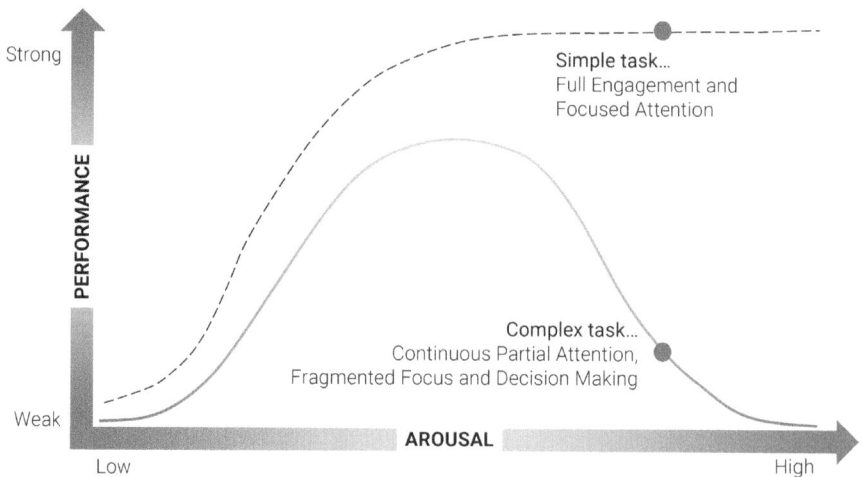

Figure 2: The arousal curve

There's no average point at which the curve slopes down and performance is impaired. It's person specific and when this personal threshold is exceeded and an individual tipping point has been reached, growth ends and the person will start to experience negative stress (Goud & Krane 1992). There is, therefore, a pressure 'sweet spot'. You'll most likely be able to recall moments in your own experience where the previously energising buzz of busyness stopped and the beginning of energy-depleting stress took its place.

We use a simplified version of the Yerkes–Dodson curve in our consulting (Figure 3). We find it helps individuals and their managers relate the curve to their own experience and start thinking about how pressure and performance might be correlated in their own part of the business. We ask them to consider where they and their team members might place themselves now, what the general direction of travel might be and, most importantly, what factors might influence how fast people move from left to right. We also ask them to consider how long people can stay in the high performance stretch zone before they risk wellbeing and performance by slipping into the strain and overwhelmed regions of the curve. In asking these questions we are, of course, nudging them towards discovering that the key to sustainability of organisational performance is intentional recovery at the individual level.

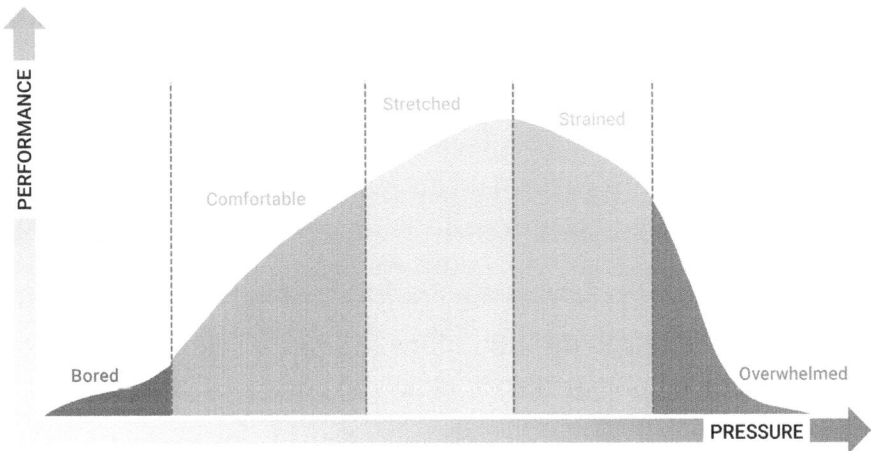

Figure 3: Pressure performance curve

The pressure performance curve and recovery

As careers develop, workplace responsibilities tend to increase and not always in a linear fashion. As the demands on your time and energy rise and conflict, the internal stories you build about your need to respond can become more intense, persistent and loud, frequently pushing you to redirect time away from other areas of your life that also matter to you. Earlier on in your career, you can slowly build confidence as you do well, get great feedback and start to feel a bit more comfortable – secure that 'you've got this' and have the skills and experience needed to do the job. This is your comfort zone and it's a great place to be. You might stay here for a while, cruising along, until external pressures increase – perhaps because of a change in leadership or other unfamiliar factors such as new technology or a sudden increase in process or product complexity. When this happens, you're bounced out of your comfort zone. This, like Rabbi Twerski's lobster, is the stimulus for growth and your capabilities need to be extended by meeting unfamiliar challenges that require skills you haven't yet perfected. This is uncomfortable because it's unfamiliar. Humans like predictability and familiarity and are quite risk averse because anything new could be perceived as dangerous. This is the reason why change creates so much discomfort and why it's often the case that necessity is the mother of invention – the only way through it is through it. Being forced to adapt and find new ways of responding adds to your stock of coping skills and capabilities and this forms the basis of personal growth. In this way it's possible to see how the Yerkes–Dodson arousal principle works on a day to day basis, as pressure both creates the conditions for and accelerates personal development, helping people to make the best use of their personal resources and even extend them.

So far, so good. This is surely the route to doing more with less – we just keep growing, right? In theory, yes, but human brains are not blobs of solder on a circuit – they construct dynamic organic algorithms. Our poor Stone Age brains are doing their valiant best to process the daily bombardment of 'data' from the outside world. The truth is, though, they get worn out by the constant push/pull exchange that exists between the risk-averse ancient brain and the more rational 'you've got this, it'll be OK' part of the brain, which is bigger and newer and hovers over your eyes. This will be explored more in the next chapter but it's this 'battle of the brains' that's largely responsible for burnout – a condition that anyone can find themselves in if too much time is spent in the strain zone. Continuous personal development can only happen under specific circumstances, the most important being regular intentional oscillation between contribution and recovery – energy out balanced with energy in. What that means by reference to the model and the questions we ask our workshop participants is that as long as you deliberately create opportunities for renewal, you can stay in the stretch zone almost indefinitely.

The practice of intentional recovery is a key modifiable factor in keeping pressure and stress separate from each other and *the* enabler for sustainable, healthy high performance. Despite this it seems to get very little company airtime and is often misunderstood as a concept. This intentional act is seen by some as unproductive time, or even slacking. We once worked with a line manager who stuck his head out of a window that overlooked the space in which his team were taking a workshop recovery break and shouted words to the effect of 'Hey, you lot! What are you all doing out there? Haven't you got any work to do?' Presumably the thought was that more progress towards objectives would be made by going back to the office for 15 minutes or staying in the training room and catching up on emails. This exchange was as funny at the time as it was extreme but it does illustrate how some people view the value of recovery. Unfortunately, seeing recovery time as unproductive or wasteful is to fundamentally misunderstand the mechanism of sustainable performance in the first place. As mentioned earlier on, humans aren't designed to always be 'on'. Promoting and supporting intentional recovery in the team is one of the most productive and strategic tools in a manager's toolbox, equipping teams to use pressure to their advantage, avoid stress and keep developing and growing. It's a route to sustainable high performance, yet it's often not used or rejected as an option because of outdated narratives such as 'I must always be seen to be working' or, through fear of negative judgement, 'My boss wouldn't like it if I took a break'. Failure to recognise the human need for recovery is to the detriment of both employee wellbeing and organisational performance.

Ultradian rhythms

Human beings function cyclically on a circadian, 24-hour body clock cycle. But within that cycle there are secondary cycles known as ultradian rhythms – shorter waves cycling every 90–120 minutes whereby certain physical needs are required to be met. These needs will include moving around to get more oxygenated blood circulating through the body and will possibly also involve the need to hydrate, eat or use the toilet. We are therefore wired through this rhythm to attempt to recover the energy expended in the preceding 90–120 minutes. The body is fully tuned in to its physical needs – in fact it's the only thing it has any interest in. This being the case, it automatically ascertains what it needs and always attempts to fulfil those needs. You need only think about your ability to concentrate in a Teams meeting if you need to use the toilet. Your brain will be intently focusing on the most opportune moment to absent yourself, not on what the speaker is saying. Next time you're in a face to face meeting that goes on for more than 90 minutes, play 'yawn and leg bounce bingo'. See how many people you notice – and include yourself in this – stifling yawns, involuntarily stretching or moving their feet around under the desk. These are the bodies that are rightly attempting to meet their own physical needs.

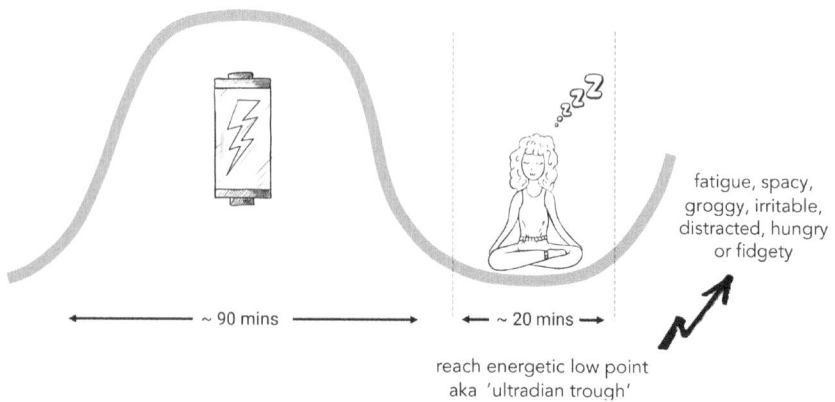

~ 90 mins
~ 20 mins

fatigue, spacy, groggy, irritable, distracted, hungry or fidgety

reach energetic low point aka 'ultradian trough'

Figure 4: An ultradian wave

It doesn't matter how interested you are in the subject matter or how mission critical it seems, the body will try to get its primary needs met. At the same time social or workplace conventions work to suppress or ignore its requests – we mostly feel we can't get up in the middle of a meeting to do star jumps or otherwise improve blood to the major muscle groups. When ignored in this way the body naturally finds workarounds. These may take many forms, among them lower concentration or slower, less creative cognition. Without exception, they all come with negative energy and performance consequences. A global marketing manager for a large, fast-moving consumer goods company once shared that, as a badge of honour, team members would compete to see who could hold their bladder the longest during all-day meetings. Such musty views are as unproductive as they are physically damaging.

By intentionally recovering our energy every 90–120 minutes and working with the body's ultradian rhythms, employees give themselves the best opportunity to sustain a high level of performance and be at their optimum for most of the day. Far from being unproductive, time spent recovering is a time investment that both fuels and enhances the next performance wave. This should be practised in a 'short periods, many times' format as opposed to working flat out for four hours and then taking an hour off (we recommend 10 minutes in every 90). The best news of all is that this wellbeing and performance-enhancing activity requires absolutely no capital investment and is freely available to everyone, anywhere in the company.

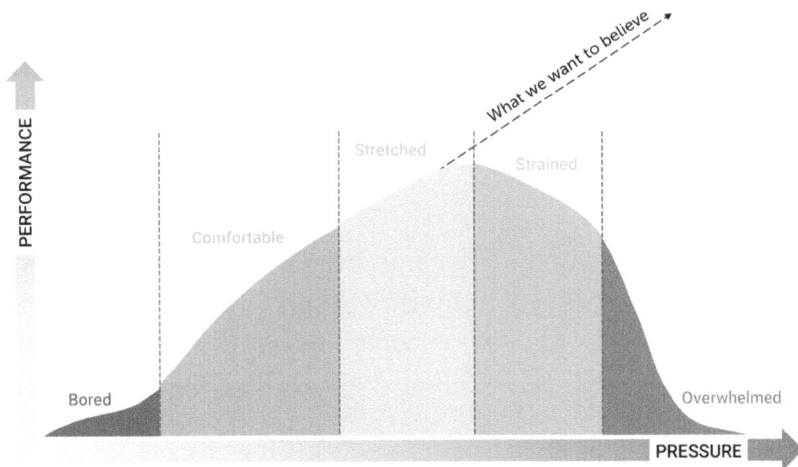

Figure 5: The pressure performance relationship as we would prefer it

If something that beneficial to your wellbeing and performance was free in a store you'd probably be tempted to grab some – and yet despite this people don't put focused time into recovery. Intuitively we know performance degrades over time – and bodies also send signals to help us notice – but at the root of this behaviour is a belief that says 'just keep on keeping on'. It works better for you to imagine that, as long as you go a little faster and get a bit more done via small efficiencies and adjustments, then you can keep your personal performance curve rising indefinitely and stay on top of everything.

We have a technical term for this idea: fantasy. As much as we'd prefer to believe otherwise, this type of personal sustainability is not achievable without regular and intentional recovery. It's the persistent tendency to regard time dedicated to recovery as unproductive that deters employees from choosing to build this valuable activity into their working day – aided of course by the fact that no one else is doing it either. Despite feeling that it might be a good idea to step into a renewal space, people's learned behaviour is to autofill that space with another task – a bit more doing. Checking emails and replying to messages are the most frequent default, fitting well as they do into the little spaces between bigger tasks or meetings. It feels productive and efficient to spend these small spaces 'getting ahead' or 'staying on top' but ironically doing so actually undermines personal performance even if you believe it's being boosted.

The zero-sum game gone wrong

The more/less quadrant model tells us that cumulative work and life demands and the way they're combining to amplify the effects are fast exceeding the collective capacity to cope. To meet the 'more' on the right, employees have been forced to reappropriate resources from the left, which has worked well in keeping the corporate boats afloat. In fact it's likely that some businesses may only be sustaining their current growth rate by adopting this method. They are effectively trading on the goodwill of staff to not only use every minute of every day for delivery but also to supplement that with a fair number of unpaid recovery hours afterwards.

Achieving more of one thing to the detriment of another is a zero-sum. However, it stops being a zero-sum when one of the factors is actively damaged in the process. Achieving more but at the expense of time and attention allocated to items in the 'less' column is the equivalent of living in a house on stilts and using the stilts to make a fire to keep you warm. It's a clear sustainability issue. However, the corporate belief still seems to be that if employers can just find a way to release it, find a mechanism that enables people to work smarter, squeeze out the inefficiencies and make better use of enabling technology, there's a bit more capacity to be had. But as Simon Sinek says in his 2019 talk, 'Trusting teams: the 5 practices', people aren't towels: you don't wring them out to see how much you can get out of them. Doing more with less is not in itself a problem – but it becomes a problem if it's achieved by creating a situation where human beings are prevented from allocating the right amount of energy to the areas that would actually make 'more' a possibility.

No time to recover – Angela's story

Feeling unable to cope presents itself in many ways. Angela is a dynamic young manager who understands the concept and benefits of taking short recovery breaks throughout the day. However, she's so emotionally on the edge that she can't contemplate taking even five minutes out of her day to recover. Her workload is so extreme and her internal narrative about not missing a deadline so intense that she's prepared to work 12–14 hours every day, often six and sometimes even seven days a week because, she says, 'Failure is not an option.' Her days are jam packed with back to back virtual meetings and her evenings are spent catching up on emails. It's been this way for the past 18 months with no end in sight. She's unaware that her emotions are just below the surface and that they can be heard in her strained voice, the sharpness of her words and her evident irritation at having to take time out of her schedule to talk about what she believes to be 'unproductive' topics. Already admittedly overwhelmed, she lacks the connection with how she's attempting to cope with her workload, her reduced cognitive capacity and her lack of emotional regulation. *This is a woman fast-tracking to stress, sacrificing her wellbeing on the altar of her organisation's purpose.* Yet her internal narrative tells her to just keep going – clearer water is up ahead. She has closed the door on any possibility that she might do things differently, even if those behavioural adaptations would help her sustain, or even improve, her performance.

No time for family – Jeremy's story

In Chapter 1 we mentioned large trees and taproots and the necessity of spreading root systems to anchor and nourish. For some people we've worked with it's not just fine roots that get truncated; the largest ones are prevented from growing. Jeremy was a senior manager in a global pharmaceutical company. When asked if he had children, his response was 'At my level, you can't afford the luxury of a family.' When asked what he meant, he explained that in his organisation senior managers were expected to 'live to work'. Wondering if this was a personal narrative rather than a pervasive one, we facilitated a conversation among the senior HR cohort about such a viewpoint. To our surprise, it was felt to be true and actively supported. Few people, even the most highly functioning among us, want to have 'I wish I had worked harder' inscribed on their headstone. Most people will say that in the final analysis, friends and family matter the most (even while admitting there's currently a mismatch in terms of the proportion of time and energy spent with them). Family and friends can make the day to day pressures feel more comfortable and worthwhile – they can enrich and nourish our lives and provide the support network that enables us to be resilient in the face of life's storms. A corporate culture that promotes and celebrates this type of root stunting in any cohort, let alone the most senior, is most definitely a zero-sum gone wrong.

Blurred or non-existent boundaries

Having to ensure a high-quality response to conflicting personal and company objectives is mentally, emotionally and practically exhausting. The apparent impossibility of doing so is the reason why work and life boundaries have become so blurred for so many people. With no obvious way to resolve what can feel like mutually exclusive drives, the tendency is to go with the 'safer' option, which invariably means going the extra corporate mile, rather than your own purposeful ones. This is alright now and again as the modern VUCA world requires adaptability – VUCA stands for volatile, uncertain, complex, ambiguous (a term based on the work of Warren Bennis and Burt Nanus). This type of flexibility from employees can be useful. The trouble is that if repeated regularly it becomes a learned response. Diverting recovery time to meet a deadline or finish a report can quickly become a go-to strategy when the pressure is on – and the pressure is always on. Extra time enables extra work, which can then become the normal (expected) output. This means that reallocating downtime to work becomes a necessity to maintain your pace. Next time you want a moment to recover, it may appear to have an impact on your performance, which further increases the difficulty. It may look as if you're slacking off. Not wanting to appear as the slacker in the team, especially when colleagues buy into the 'just keep going' narrative, is clearly a route to trampled boundaries. When the margins between work and non-work are overlooked, colleagues and managers will be ever present in your life – at the dinner table, walking the dog, in the bathroom and even in bed at night. Meanwhile smartphones facilitate that 'always on' connection and feed the compulsion to be constantly available for work.

Sadly, a secondary (and for a while at least, invisible) effect is the simultaneous flattening of self-worth and value. When work is consistently prioritised over personal and family time, your actions devalue not only yourself but your family too. An internal war is being constantly fought between the desire to invest time and energy with those who matter most and the fear of negative consequences or judgement if you push back and say no to the demands of work. If the perception is that managers and colleagues are under the same amount of pressure and working the same long hours, then it's likely that at the crunch point our primeval need to fall in step with our colleagues will mean that we do just that. This default response is self-sustaining because few people have the time and courage to get underneath and challenge *why* it's necessary to divert time away from other aspects of life in this way. The unspoken narrative is that by not rocking the boat, you avoid a tumble into dangerous waters. In this moment it feels safer to accept likely damage to self and family than risk negative consequences at work by pushing back.

The white water analogy

In our workshops we encourage leaders to visualise the experience of pressure at work as a white water boat ride. Using the image below, we ask them to imagine a group of people in a small inflatable craft, bouncing down the rapids of a noisy and turbulent river, seeing the people in the boat as a team in their organisation.

Figure 6: The white water boat crew

In the image, if you look at their faces closely, some of the team appear anxious – focused on survival, perhaps – while the expressions of others suggest they're enjoying the thrill of the ride. The anxious-looking ones might be concerned about what's up ahead – perhaps worse is to come? Others may not have thought about or even have no idea about where they're heading or whether they'll get there safely – they're just in the moment doing what they can to keep the boat the right way up. We sometimes ask them at this point to say which one of the crew members best represents how they might be feeling in that situation, so we'll ask you to look at the picture again and do the same thing.

Our story goes on. The water is so churned up that although there are oars in the water, some people are paddling in an unhelpful way, perhaps unknowingly causing the boat to career towards a jagged rock. There may be a suspicion that a hidden rock has already hurled one team member out of the boat but nobody saw this happen because the pressure to stay upright is so great everybody is just focused on getting round the next bend.

The boat bounces on. Bends in the river mean it's impossible to see what or who is further downstream. There's a thought that maybe someone is pushing people into the water further upstream, telling them to join the others in the boat. When the boat does manage to clear the destabilising rocks, eddies and drops, having made its way safely to its destination, the wear and tear on the crew is evident. The journey was much longer than most anticipated and it has left those attempting to paddle, steer and stabilise the boat exhausted and, in some cases, emotionally burnt out. When the rapids finally peter out and the water slows (as sometimes happens in the corporate world for a week or two), those still in the boat notice that the stress and effort of the journey has changed the dynamic between them.

The boat is now rotating slowly in a pool that now feels slightly toxic – the team culture has in effect become tainted by the experience and they find themselves less comfortable with each other than they were at the start. The journey is deemed to have been a success because (nearly) everyone who set off is still in the boat. 'We expect to lose a few people on the way, right? Those of

43

us who *are* still in the boat are OK because we are still in the boat, right? We delivered the project, so we are all good.' The thing is that everyone experienced that ride differently and everyone has been altered by it – some positively, some not.

What's really going on for people?

This is, of course, all conjecture. It's just you looking at a photograph and imagining what's going on for the people in it – filling in the gaps using your natural storytelling ability and weaving a narrative about what might be going on. The point of the exercise is to illustrate just that: people use the information they have in front of them to make assumptions about what's going on now and what might happen next. This is what happens every day, in practically every interaction with colleagues, clients, friends and family. You guess and make conclusions and judgements, often by reference to only a limited amount of information, about what's going on for people. Usually you're confident that what you 'see' is what *is* going on – comfortable that what's in front of you tells you where people are with what you're saying or suggesting. The trouble is that there's a good chance some of it will not be quite right, most of the time.

We all experience the world in our own unique way. You can't know exactly what someone else is feeling about a situation, even if you're both involved in it. People only share what they want to share. What someone 'sees' in a situation and what they take out of it is unique to them, every time. Of course, you'd have a better chance of understanding their situation if they told you. However, there are many, many reasons why people don't share what they feel, think or see. You might want to but often you don't because of some low-grade concern that there might be negative consequences as a result.

In our white water analogy, few of the crew would've wanted to openly admit that they were scared or worried about a colleague they thought might have fallen out. Once on the water, it's probable that few of them felt able to share a suspicion that there might be a much better, less bumpy route to the destination. To share these insights and emotions with colleagues or leaders in this way might risk them being seen as weak, selfish or not properly committed to the team mission and identity. More damaging still, what if it were seen as evidence that they couldn't handle the pressure? Speaking up might lead to career self-sabotage.

Feeling able to share experience and insights openly requires a culture where what Amy Edmondson refers to in *The Fearless Organisation* (2018) as 'interpersonal risks' can be freely taken. If people have no reason to fear a bad outcome from openness, they're much more likely to share what could be time and resource saving insights. A culture that's safer can certainly lead to fewer unpleasant boat rides, with fewer people falling out of the boat because they've been able to share their concerns and experiences before venturing out onto the water. In this environment people can learn from each other, experiment with new ways to get things done and innovate freely. If no one feels able to say anything, guess how likely the team is to be sent down the river the same way a second time? There are obvious benefits to upskilling in order to feel able to take more interpersonal risks and be more curious about the perspectives (in other words, stories) of others. How to do this will be fully explored in later chapters but first let's look at why so many people are finding it impossible to be heard above the roar of the corporate rapids and why they're subsequently falling out of the boat in large numbers.

Chapter 2: Big questions

- ★ If you're a **team member**: what do you allow to distract you from what you're doing? How often do you find you're prioritising work over other activities that relate to your life outside of work?
- ★ If you're a **people manager**: how well do you protect your boundaries? What example do you set to those around you in relation to personal boundaries and distractions? How possible do you make it for team members to maintain a healthy separation between work and other areas of their life? Do you challenge your team members when you see their boundaries slipping?
- ★ If you're a **senior leader**: how well do you protect your boundaries? What example do you set to those around you in relation to personal boundaries and distractions? What policies do you need to implement to help support employees' choices and boundaries?

Key messages

- ★ The point of diminishing returns has been reached in relation to achieving more with the same or fewer resources. Continuing this model will worsen the existing situation, characterised by a rapidly deteriorating level of general workplace wellbeing.
- ★ Employee sustainability requires companies to set policy that moves away from a zero-sum approach of 'either/or' towards one of 'and'. Sustainable, healthy high performance can only be achieved by regular recovery, which means maintaining personal boundaries.
- ★ Feeling comfortable about speaking up and sharing how you feel is crucial for team learning and creating trust – people need to feel safe to share their insights and concerns without fear of reprisals.

3 If you can't take the heat...

The statistics on stress and mental health suggest that people who live in developed countries might be struggling with the relentless demand on their attention. These statistics serve as a sign that's hard to ignore, which is that humans can't adapt at the same rapid pace as their environment. For many people the outcome is not personal growth and development but the one that nobody wants – chronic stress.

To fully appreciate why this emotional health crisis is such a predictable outcome of how we've been living and working for the past decade, in the West at least, all that's needed is a brief look at the evolutionary past. Most people have heard of the fight, flight or freeze response and the place it occupies in our hard wiring for survival in life or death situations. However, fewer people appreciate that the same survival response is triggered when we experience continuous or even semi-permanent conflict between personal needs and professional obligations, or when the combined volume of demand from each of these sources feels bigger than the personal capacity to cope. This ancient stress response is still baked into everyone alive today and it clearly works, as it enabled ancestors to navigate existential threats long enough to give rise to everyone currently on the planet. In much the same way as it did for our ancestors, it functions to keep you safe but the world beyond our heads is now fundamentally different. This brings a dark side to an otherwise useful survival reaction.

The battle of the brains

To understand that dark side, it's necessary to consider how the human brain evolved. Primitive humans had much smaller brains – what's often called the reptilian brain. This brain contained the key elements humans needed to assess danger and ultimately survive, housed in the amygdala. The amygdala processes the information continually coming into our brains through our five senses, meting out associated emotions and perhaps triggering the fight, flight or freeze response. Primitive humans also had a mammalian brain containing the hippocampus, which is responsible for remembering specific events in our past. The amygdala and hippocampus form part of the limbic system and work together synergistically to translate our emotions into behavioural responses and form our long-term memory. This means that as primitive humans, our survival was dependent upon this emotional assessment – is this a threat to our existence, requiring a flight, fight or freeze response, or not? Evaluation of future events would be based upon past experiences. If we were attacked by a sabre-toothed tiger, not only would the fight or flight mechanism kick in but our primitive brain would also remember that such tigers are dangerous. Therefore, the next time we saw or even anticipated such a tiger, an emotional reaction would be generated, pushing us to act – fight, flight or freeze – depending upon the outcome of the previous experience, which was most likely flight.

Fast-forward to the present day and think about the continuing evolution of the human brain. The reptilian and mammalian brains still exist, yet the structure and size of the brain has changed quite dramatically. Surrounding those primitive brain structures – often colloquially known as the chimp brain – we now have the modern, human part of the brain, the neocortex. Within this, it's the prefrontal cortex (PFC) in particular that enables us to make rationalisations about the world around us. Ultimately it enables us to gain cognitive control over our responses, mediating impulse control and allowing us to think about the future rather than simply experiencing an emotion about it.

Relentless pressure from external demands, coupled with your own internal expectations, can trigger the same stress response many times during a typical day. Your rational brain has cognitive understanding that there's no real existential threat. However, your chimp brain – working at an unconscious level and processing environmental information and emotional response – reacts anyway. It releases the adrenaline and cortisol needed to adjust your physiology in readiness for fight or flight and prompts the survival-motivated emotions of fear and anxiety. These emotions are powerful and affecting by design, causing the battle between the different areas of your brain to intensify. Often the emotional response to a situation – called emotional hijacking – can be so intense that it disarms attempts by the human brain to make a more balanced assessment of the situation. The ensuing internal conflict of trying to rationalise your way out of an emotional response is exhausting, often causing the human brain to retreat and tend to its wounds.

What happens when the amygdala wins?

The more the chimp brain wins out in this way, the more the human brain is likely to side with its primeval counterpart. At this point, now meeting little or no resistance from the human brain that had previously been acting as a braking system, the chimp brain's sensitivity to perceived threats increases exponentially. With the brakes off, the fight or flight switch is repeatedly tripped forward. Each time this happens, adrenaline and cortisol flood the body, heightening our alertness, awareness and sensitivity to additional threats. The heart rate increases and capillaries constrict to divert oxygen and nutrients to the muscles and vital organs to minimise bleeding if bitten and prepare the body for escape or combat. This continuous state of arousal causes the PFC to finally wave the white flag and a state of chronic and continuous stress results.

Not surprisingly, the cascade of hormones released during a stress response prompts a range of physiological changes to occur in the body. As a powerful agent for rapid, short-term changes to blood chemistry and related physiological adaptation, it's not desirable for these chemicals to be in our bodies continuously. Over time, the constant presence of adrenaline in our circulatory system starts to impair the autoimmune system, causing adrenal fatigue and lower immunity. This direct correlation between the stress response, diminished immunity and subsequent ill health is well known and was well documented prior to the Covid-19 pandemic. However, given the huge increase in people experiencing stress and mental health issues during the pandemic period itself and doing so on an ongoing basis, this relationship has since been of even greater public health concern. Chronic stress contributes to high blood pressure and is a known factor in clinical anxiety, depression and addiction. It's also indirectly linked to obesity and has a deleterious impact on cardiovascular health as it contributes to the formation of artery-clogging deposits. Our chimp brain has little or no ability to differentiate between physical existential threats and cognitive ones. Fortunately, there are ways to wrest back control and give the human brain an opportunity to re-engage and call off the chimp brain before it prompts a reaction that is unhelpful from both an endocrine and a social perspective.

The process just described has big implications for workplace wellbeing and performance and to see why we should revisit how it is that human brains enable their owners to make sense of the world around them.

The face model

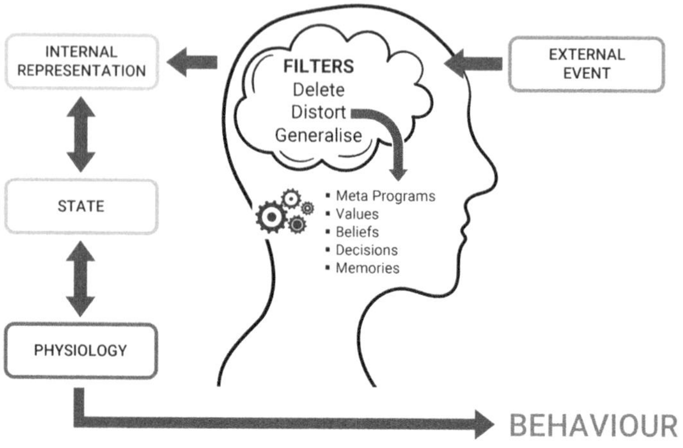

Figure 1: The face model

All day, every day, external stimuli from your external environment enter your brain via your senses, most of which you don't experience at a conscious level. There's so much 'data' that your conscious brain couldn't possibly process it all, so most of this information is effectively filtered out and deleted (try to remember every word you've read in this chapter so far). The information that your brain tends to hang on to is novel or unfamiliar, as there are clear survival benefits in picking up a 'rustle in the bushes' and singling out such stimuli for further scrutiny. Unusual information needs to be processed so it's passed through your own individual set of filters. They're unique to you because they were honed through the interaction of your memories, past experience, education and upbringing and the related value and belief systems. In a sense they play a big part in making up your individual personality. Importantly, these screening tools are also intertwined with your behavioural preferences – what are known as your meta programs. If you've ever used a personality profiling tool you may already have insight into what your own cognitively coded preferences are.

What's noticed and retained is then interpreted using these unique filters so that you can make sense of the information you're receiving. Brains love patterns and are primed to use them not only to look for divergence from what's already 'known' but also to interpret what appears to be new and therefore unknown, using our unique filters almost as decryption keys, decoding the data input through our five senses into something usable. In this way 'new' is deciphered by reference to stored knowledge about 'older'. On a practical level this means we make sense of what's happening to us now and what that means by generalising about it. For example, 'This *always* happens to me.' Our confirmation bias then confounds the interpretation of future events so that they fall in line with the belief created by the generalisation. Doing this has enormous benefits for cognitive efficiency because the brain can make optimal use of limited internal energy resources. Certainly, having to work out what something is and what to do with it every time you experience it would be chaotic and highly inefficient. However, like many things that look good at first glance, there's a snag. When it comes to stress, this autonomic tendency to generalise can quickly work against us. Our hyper-aroused brain needs only a whiff of something familiarly negative to conclude that this new event is also a threat, prompting a potentially unnecessary and wasteful stress response.

Once external data has been generalised in this way – negatively or positively – we effectively create an internal story around it. As we saw in Chapter 1, humans are natural storytellers and the stories we tell ourselves and each other hold powerful sway over our emotions. It's hardly surprising that our brains have evolved to support this behaviour – since around 30,000 BC 'the oral tradition' has been the mechanism by which humans have communicated ideas and shaped local cultures. The role of storytelling can be seen in primitive cave drawings depicting rituals and hunting scenes, passing stories down through the centuries. As any student of literature will tell you, the consistency of thematic preoccupations inside fairy stories indicates that cautionary and culture-shaping narratives have been around for a very long time.

Because our stories are permeated by strong emotions and the human brain is primed to be vigilant for threats, you can be blindsided by your stories and stuck inside negative feedback loops. What you tell yourself about something, often shaped by generalisation, directly impacts what you feel about that thing. Your internal interpretation of the world around you triggers an emotional response. Emotions change your physiology and drive what you do next. If your internal story and the emotions that accompany it are negative, the behavioural response will most likely be avoidant or confrontational, escalating the negatives. Any hope of learning how to deal with the triggering situation more effectively will be lost. This lack of learning goes on to preserve the initial perception of the negative story, creating a more intense negative loop which goes on to both validate the original story and remove any opportunity to update it and break the cycle.

Unfortunately for those experiencing chronic stress, this isn't the only negative impact of unhelpful internal stories. Once 'stuck' in a negative emotional state with chimp and human brains colluding, the ability to step back from these emotions and the drama that accompanies this interpretation of the event diminishes. This makes it much more difficult to even consider if there might be alternative interpretations or responses available. When this happens, your focus becomes myopic and you're prevented from seeing a broader perspective. Often the person is so locked into their narrative, so shut off from any potential wider angle on their situation, that they're unaware of what's happening to them and unable to recognise warning signs that are clearly visible to others. It's easy to see why people caught up in this type of negative feedback loop won't readily access any wellbeing support that might be available to them as they don't yet know they need it.

The Emotional Dip

When 'stuck' in the dip, it can impact our mental health, wellbeing, and performance

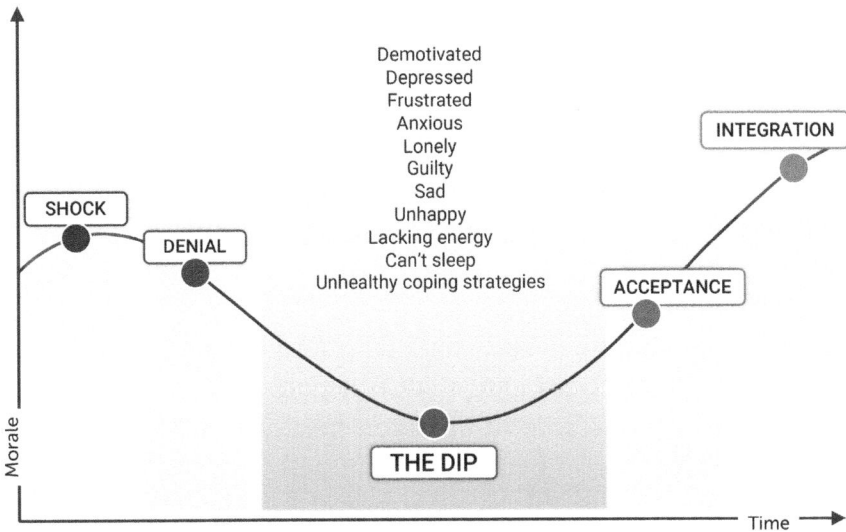

Figure 2 The emotional dip (inspired by Kubler-Ross)

The Kubler-Ross change curve (1969) is a useful model to describe what happens when people get caught in negative feedback loops such as those that occur during chronic stress. When unlooked-for events occur and following the initial shock and denial, there's a slump, manifesting in negative emotions. Typically people stay here for a while before accepting the situation, climbing their way out of the negative emotional slump and integrating new ways of responding. However, with continuous negative feedback loops, you're more prone to longer periods in 'the dip' (see Figure 2), as those feedback loops can affect your confidence and ability to accept and integrate. Couple this with the failure of any previous attempt at doing things differently to propel you towards acceptance and you may find yourself sliding back down into the dip, further intensifying the negative emotions. This is an extremely vulnerable place to be, not only in terms of personal performance but, as we shall see, in terms of susceptibility to be drawn into 'drama', taking things personally that aren't directed toward you, along with a higher risk of burnout.

We must say at this point that internal narratives in themselves are not a problem. Many of the stories you tell yourself can be very useful – not least because they're the basis of the same values and belief systems that keep you on track with your personal purpose. They also help you connect directly with the aims and objectives of the company you work for. In fact, your human brain is very good at creating the higher mission and purpose ideals that are fundamental to what's often described as the human spirit. The murkier side of storytelling rests in the chimp brain's survival-based fondness for negativity over positivity – for sniffing out and responding to threats of any size, far more readily than it does a success story. At the slightest sniff of personal risk, the chimp brain's preference will be to abandon the mission ship, overrun higher order ideals and overwrite them with a darker instruction – stay still and quiet; this situation or this person/these people don't have your back; you're not safe here. This is the reason why background anxiety about the potential for personal negative consequences at work can be so damaging to employee wellbeing and performance. Continuous perception of low-grade threats eats into your employees' psyches, resulting in an uninterrupted state of personal fear, which downgrades performance and dials up poor mental health.

There's no place for emotions at work, right?

It does sound as if the stress problem would be alleviated if people brought less emotion into work with them. Indeed, it used to be said that 'there's no place at work for emotions'. There's obviously less support for this sentiment now than was the case even a decade ago. However, there are still a few who would prefer it if we kept 'feelings' out of the day to day business of running a business. Inconveniently for those of this persuasion, humans are emotional beings. Most of what motivates people to get up and keep 'doing' is rooted in one or more emotions – driving the 'just keep going' response experienced by most members of staff when they're buffeted by distractions, conflicting demands and relentless pressure.

When we talk about employee engagement, we're clearly referring to employees being emotionally engaged with both the task and the company objectives. Given how popular employee engagement has become as a modifiable performance factor, all employers are obviously banking on a fair bit of emotional connection. Indeed, this association between work and emotional connection has become a prerequisite in the modern, leaner workforce, facilitating as it does the continuity of contribution necessary when colleagues are displaced. After downsizing or attrition, most employees still in post care enough about the outcome to find a way to meet the mission, even if it means shouldering more of the burden themselves. Work is a hotbed of emotion and while there's often a lot of hope, joy, pride and excitement to be had at the office or factory, it's also less happily often accompanied by anger, sadness, shame, frustration and, as we have just demonstrated, fear.

What are emotions?

Given their importance, we should take a moment to consider what emotions are. There's currently no scientific consensus regarding the definition of an emotion but 'an instinctive or intuitive feeling as distinguished from reasoning or knowledge' is typical. There's a broader consensus that emotions are mental states brought on by neurophysiological changes and variously associated with a degree of either pleasure or displeasure. What prompts them into being are three important hormones – noradrenaline, dopamine and serotonin, which blend in differing combinations to create the basic emotions listed above.

Because these hormones create emotions, they therefore come from inside the body – mostly from the hypothalamus and pituitary glands in the brain, working together to signal to other endocrine glands in the body to make hormones that affect and protect every aspect of human health (Endocrine Society 2022). As a result, another person can't actually give you an emotion. No matter how you perceive a situation or person, your internal representation of what's going on outside your head triggers your emotions. Whether you're triggered or not depends on what your narrative looks like. For example, why does one person fear spiders while another does not? You may be thinking that the answer lies in learned behaviour and you'd be partially correct. This is because when you were young, you learned how others reacted and subsumed that behaviour as your own. However, you must still create your own internal story for your emotions to be triggered.

What's most important to note here is that emotions will be present in every response. Emotions sit at the unconscious level as part of the chimp brain. They're not conscious thoughts or decisions. We don't consciously decide to be happy or sad. Emotions are the reaction to the story of what we're thinking or doing. Neither is there such a thing as a 'bad' emotion in and of itself – all emotions provide valuable information in helping us survive. If we feel anxious, we may take steps to avoid situations linked to a negative story. If we feel happy, we'll generally gravitate towards doing more of the activity that creates a positive story. What's essential when it comes to the stories we create and how we perceive the world is being aware that emotions exist and using this awareness to practise emotional regulation. This is the ability to recognise a negative narrative, understand the associated negative emotion and deliberately change the internal story to trigger a different, more positive, emotion. This opens the door to consciously being able to choose more beneficial behavioural responses. The wellbeing and performance benefits of helping employees to do more of this should be pretty clear.

Blame

Blame is a specific behavioural response and one that can feel liberating, mainly because it alleviates us from having to take responsibility for our own responses. Little wonder then that blame is so popular! If you place yourself firmly in the role of the persecuted, effectively pointing the finger at the persecutor, you can project all your negativity towards them. Few people are sufficiently self-aware to be able to see themselves doing this but most people do it at some stage or another. It goes without saying that this unconscious strategy is ineffective and usually ensures that you stay stuck in blame mode, believing yourself powerless to change anything. This makes you feel worse, leading you to ramp up the intensity of your projected emotions, which tends to make the situation deteriorate further. After a time – as all that negativity is so exhausting – you run out of energy to keep feeling negative and at that level you stop projecting it. However, that doesn't mean the negativity has gone – it simply means you've just run out of energy to externalise it. This is a dangerous place to be, as the body can't maintain this level of intense negative emotion indefinitely. When you suppress negative emotions, you're effectively internalising them – turning them inwards on yourself. This is the slow sleepwalk into burnout and from here there are only a few small steps to a more serious mental health issue.

At this point, it's worth remembering that those internal battles mentioned earlier – wanting to spend time with those who matter the most yet fearing negative consequences or narratives such as 'I want to do this, yet I don't feel I can' or 'It's really important to be a great parent, yet I really want to be a great manager' – are all rooted in strong emotions and extremely draining. Those either/or struggles, those I should/shouldn't narratives that we all continually try to resolve, end up leaving us at risk of being emotionally drained at best, chronically stressed with physical and mental health issues at worst.

Overwhelmed and overwound – the human cost

The only positive aspect of the increase in cases of stress during the past decade is that people are at least talking about them. Conversations about stress and mental health have moved out of the shadows and into the light. This is important progress as a greater understanding of cause and effect can lead to more meaningful conversations about where stress comes from and the different ways in which it can affect people. However, talking openly about the symptoms and causes does nothing to reduce incidence if the talking doesn't include strategies to address the sources. Open dialogue can be used to attract leadership attention and from there catalyse important conversations about the many ways in which stress eats into employee health, performance and ultimately business profits.

A secondary effect of increased openness about the topic is that attitudes towards stress have changed. It's now less often seen as a sign of weakness or, conversely, as a badge of commitment – a kind of observable evidence of more highly evolved engagement with the company's purpose. The stress response is neither of these – just a hard-wired neurophysiological response that stems from the core of what makes us human.

Stress and mental health

In physiological terms the structure of our brain hasn't changed all that much in the past several hundred thousand years but our environment, social conditions and pace of life have changed beyond all recognition. The truth is that life is changing at a faster rate than our brains can cope with. The brain's in-built plasticity that enables a baby to be born anywhere in the world and absorb the cultural development instructions supplied by its environment means that brains can and do adapt. However, the process takes time. When the stimulus changes, brains initiate their own software upgrades yet the upload takes a bit longer than on your smartphone. For our purposes, we should acknowledge the current workplace stress epidemic as evidence of that struggle taking place. It shouldn't be taken in any way to be a deficiency – rather an ongoing process of employee adaptation in response to a rapidly changing environment. The pandemic years saw a dramatic increase in the negative effect on people's mental health. The Global Burden of Diseases estimates a 28 per cent increase in depression and a 26 per cent increase in anxiety in one year post pandemic. To put that into perspective, pre pandemic, 193 million people had a major depressive disorder, increasing to 246 million, and 298 million people had anxiety disorders, increasing to 374 million post pandemic (see healthdata.org/gbd and WHO 2022). Many of those people were still feeling the effects long after lockdowns eased. This serves as a good illustration of just how rapidly mental wellbeing can decline when events feel out of our personal control.

The mental wellbeing continuum

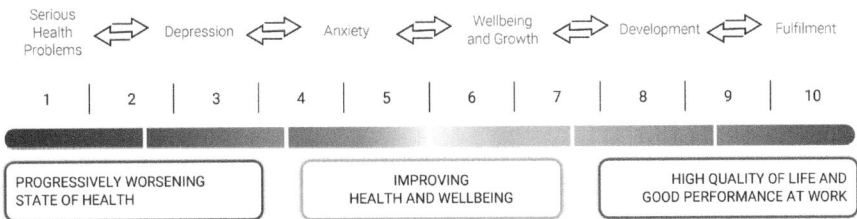

Figure 3: The mental wellbeing continuum (inspired by Teasdale/Heron)

If mental wellbeing can be seen as existing on a continuum with very good on the right-hand end and very poor on the left, then the stress response should be marked as left of the midpoint. In our view, in such a model stress needs to be seen as existing to the left of centre because there's no such thing as 'positive stress'. When people use this term what they usually mean is 'positive pressure'. We call this a 'Goldilocks zone' of external stimulus that sharpens awareness and focus and gets us ready for action – enough stimulus to make you energised, engaged, fully alive and up for a challenge.

It's a 'when the going gets tough' type of idea with enough pressure to stimulate an engaged and alert response but not so much that you're in cognitive fight or flight mode.

If we're to call into question a startlingly prevalent narrative that some stress is to be expected and even encouraged on the grounds that it's good for performance, it's an important distinction. These complex changes come at a high cost when repeated regularly. It's an unhelpful and potentially damaging conflation of the terms pressure and stress. As a reminder, the former is a neutral input that can produce positive or negative outcomes; the latter is a negative outcome. As you now know, a full-blown stress response triggers powerful hormones that drive the rapid change in blood chemistry needed to support the physical exertion needed for combat or escape. You know these complex changes also come at a high cost to health when repeated regularly. It's no surprise then that stress is a factor in a large number of mental health issues, including depression (reduced mood and interest) and anxiety (excessive or persistent anticipation of a future threat) (Bonde 2008).

The Health and Safety Executive estimates that nearly one in six people of working age have a diagnosable mental health issue (HSE 2022). However, due to the culture of silence that still exists in many companies, the leadership is effectively insulated from the true extent of the issue – although, it should be noted, they're not personally immune. We once worked with the senior leaders of an engineering company, one of whom was keen to show full support 'for about 90 per cent' of our views on pressure and performance. However, he went to some trouble to point out that the other 10 per cent would mean that employees – already working a 12-hour shift – would not be available for overtime, thus losing around eight full-time employee equivalents. This would lead to an unacceptable slowdown in production. No amount of persuasion helped him to see an alternative perspective. However, two years later, at another resilience workshop we ran for managers, he publicly advocated everything we said, admitting his previous view had been naive. When asked why he'd had a change in attitude, he explained that he himself had suffered burnout and had been off work with stress. His lived experience meant he could now relate directly to the notion that stress is the negative outcome of pressure and, if not addressed, it has devastating effects on both physical and mental health and performance.

Employees have many reasons for concealing their stress and inner turmoil from colleagues and bosses. Among these is the fear of being seen as weak or unreliable or unfit for promotion. We'll be revisiting why this is and what you might be able to do about it in later chapters. Programmes such as the Time to Talk campaign by Rethink Mental Illness (rethink.org/get-involved/awareness-days-and-events/time-to-talk-day) or the Work Right campaign by the HSE (workright.campaign.gov.uk) have done much to encourage employees to talk about what they're experiencing. However, the number of people not talking still vastly outweighs the number who feel able to speak up about how they're feeling. Furthermore, those suffering from a mental health disorder may experience psychosocial disability, arising when a person with long-term mental impairment experiences barriers hindering their ability to fully and effectively participate equally with others in society, such as discrimination, exclusion and stigma (WHO 2022).

As a small but relevant sidebar, research carried out by psychologist Jamie Whitehouse suggests that human stress behaviours may have evolved as a communication tool to aid social cohesion. His work raises the question of whether external stress behaviours in humans serve a similar function to that of primates, where signalling stress seems to function as an avoidance of conflict (Whitehouse et al 2017). This lack of acceptance and openness about the legitimacy and inevitability of the stress response might be fuelling even greater disconnection between colleagues and managers. As a social species our ancestors took their cues from each other. As modern humans, we've become so enthralled by our performance and professional progression that we've forgotten to value human wellbeing as well as the legitimacy of shielding work–life boundaries to protect it. Many companies we work with seem to display a culture of 'every man or woman for themselves', even though research suggests that we're wired to communicate and share, not hide, our struggles so that others in the group can benefit. In other words, not feeling able to talk about our stress and emotional health adds to both short-term distress and the longer-term incidence.

The bottom line is that most people affected by workplace stress don't feel comfortable talking about the psychological or physiological effects they're experiencing. This means that the employer remains ignorant of the damage to their human assets as well as the contribution and profitability that's leached away through all that distress. A true lose–lose situation. Let's take a brief look at some of those human and commercial losses.

The psychological and physical effects of stress

The impact on an individual's psychological health is obviously the most evident consequence of work-related stress. On a psychological level, employees suffering from work-related stress are likely to experience symptoms of common mental health issues such as anxiety and depression. These symptoms can be serious and far reaching and, as you can see from the tables in Figure 4 below, produce outcomes in several different dimensions – emotionally, cognitively, physically and behaviourally.

PSYCHOLOGICAL	PHYSICAL	BEHAVIOURAL
Anxiety	Aches and pains	
Depression	Diarrhea	
Excessive fear	Constipation	
Excessing worry	Increased heart rate	Repetitive compulsive behaviour
Impatience	Palpitations and chest pains	
On edge	Loss of libido	Mood swings
Mind racing	Frequent colds or flu	Change in eating habits
Irritable	Hypertension	Withdraw socially
Nervous	Headaches	Stop exercising
Indecisive	Migraines	Unhelpful coping strategies: excessive drinking, smoking, working
Poor concentration	Tense tight muscles	
Poor memory	Hyperventilation	
Vivid dreams	Acne	Restless
Feeling overwhelmed	Nausea	Angry outbursts
Lack of motivation	Low energy and fatigue	
Feeling sad	Unable to sleep	
Panicky	Sweating	
	Asthma	

Figure 4: Psychological, physical and behavioural effects of stress

Stress is therefore made manifest in many immediate short-term psychological and physiological outcomes but it also affects the body in more fundamental ways. It can have a profound impact on the nervous system. Most of us will have experienced the tension headaches or even migraines that are rooted in our psychological response to persistent stressors but there are more dramatic ways in which the nervous system can be affected. It can be the root cause of much more severe problems, for example seizures and vision loss. A recent report found that ongoing stress and the attendant high levels of cortisol are risk factors in both the development and progression of deteriorating vision (Sabel et al 2018). We've worked with a senior manager in a global engineering company who completely lost his sight due to stress. He was off work for a year, not knowing throughout whether he'd be able to work again. He regained some of his sight after this period but his vision was permanently damaged so he took a slightly lower-level management position, knowing this was the right thing to do for his health and wellbeing. Psychologically, however, he felt like a failure, felt judged and felt as if he was letting everyone down. This man's extended stress response took a heavy toll on both his physical and psychological health.

Another unfortunate consequence of stress relates to fertility. Any couple trying to conceive will have been told that stress can lead to a drop in fertility as well as sex drive. Researchers attribute much of the stress effect on sexual function to an increase in the stress hormones cortisol and adrenaline. As explained by Daniela Kaufer, a UC Berkeley assistant professor of integrative biology, it's adaptive not to waste resources on reproduction during times of acute stress, shutting down reproduction for 24 hours or so until the stress has gone. These functions go back a long way in terms of human evolution (ScienceDaily 2009).

Cardiovascular consequences

One extremely serious consequence of chronic stress can be the increased risk of damage to the cardiovascular system, such as cardiovascular disease, coronary artery disease and cardiac arrest (Tennant 2000). As we age, our arteries naturally calcify, reducing in diameter and therefore in capacity to carry oxygenated blood around the body (Pandya 1998). The resulting heart rate increase is in response to the need for a consistent supply of oxygenated blood and a greater force of blood through the narrowed arteries. This increases blood pressure and the risk of either stroke or heart attack. Additionally, rumination over events and worrying about the personal consequences of them can cause exaggerated and prolonged increases in our blood pressure and heart rate, further contributing to hypertension over time (Hassoun et al 2015).

Immunological consequences

Adrenaline and cortisol, which are released by our adrenal glands during the stress response, are extremely powerful and trigger a long list of physiological changes in the body. You'll remember that hormones this potent aren't designed to be in your bloodstream continuously and that when they are they put a strain on the immune and tissue repair systems, with predictable physical health consequences. If the body believes it's in a life or death situation (again, the brain doesn't discriminate between physical and non-physical threats as far as triggering a response is concerned), it diverts resources away from what are temporarily considered non-essential tasks. This is so that all available resources can be focused on the immediate threat. This makes sense – there's no need to hold back resources to repair a bitten leg if the rest of you gets eaten by the predator. A better resource management strategy for the body is to direct resources to evade capture in the first instance and worry about healing a bit later. You may have noticed that when you've been stressed for a few days you're more susceptible to colds and stomach bugs. Your body is trying to protect you, yet paradoxically, because of the suppression of the autoimmune system, it's making you more vulnerable (Morey et al 2015). Stress weakens the immune system and makes us more susceptible to everyday bugs and novel ones. There's a definite correlation between short-term sickness absence and stress – people aren't necessarily avoiding work but their response to work has made them vulnerable to illness.

Consequences for sleep

It's common knowledge that work-related stress hinders sleep. Most of us have experienced being 'tired but wired' at the end of the day. There's no shortage of research exploring how the quality and quantity of our sleep is impacted by external factors. One particularly interesting study examined the impacts of known work-related stressors on sleep quality indicators (Fortunato & Harsh 2006). Overall, the results demonstrated that job stressors directly and interactively affect sleep quality for affected individuals. Additional studies have explored the extent to which low sleep quality impacts stress levels and job performance, pointing to another circular relationship – stress hinders sleep while lack of sleep increases stress. Yet another collection of studies looked at six domains of what's known as 'occupational functioning', namely absenteeism, workplace mistakes or accidents, productivity, job satisfaction and career progression. Insomnia symptoms were consistently associated with increased absence from work – elevated workplace accidents, reduced productivity, inhibited career progression and weakened job satisfaction (Kucharczyk et al 2012). Additionally, and critically, there's the risk associated with driving while drowsy. An estimated 72,000 deaths per annum occur in this way. The cognitive effect of lack of sleep on reaction speeds and judgement of distance is thought to be as great, if not greater, than they are in driving under the influence of alcohol. Remember, we spend around a third of our lives sleeping and it forms the physical, emotional and mental foundation needed for making the other two thirds of our lives successful, rewarding and energised. It's certainly not a waste of time.

Other physical consequences of stress

According to the NHS, teeth grinding and jaw clenching, known technically as bruxism, is another common physical manifestation of stress or anxiety (nhs.uk/conditions/teeth-grinding). As a secondary consequence, some sufferers then go on to experience facial pain and headaches and it can seriously wear down the teeth over time. Stress can also induce ulcers – common acute erosive or ulcerative lesions – in the stomach or the mouth. Other common consequences of stress include digestive problems such as indigestion, heartburn, constipation and diarrhoea; skin problems such as alopecia, psoriasis and rashes; and feeling nauseous or fatigued and having trouble breathing.

Secondary health effects

The conditions mentioned above are specific health concerns for many. However, chronic stress is often the driving force behind an individual engaging in harmful behaviours that act as coping mechanisms for what feels like relentless demand, distraction and pressure. These harmful behaviours might include overeating, smoking, recreational drug use or the overconsumption of alcohol. We might also add overworking and compensatory over-exercising to that list too. Such addictive behaviours can lead to further health and social disruptions which, by complicating or damaging relationships and or work performance, amplify the underlying issue.

Burnout

We hear the term burnout a lot, although it isn't all that well understood in physiological terms. Put simply, the long-term effects of repeated triggering of the fight or flight response inflicts disruptive complications on the autonomic nervous system. Among them is adrenal fatigue, whereby the adrenal glands cease releasing adrenaline 'on cue', leading to chronic lethargy and a lack of motivation and energy. These extremes of anxiety and fatigue combine to create burnout (Salvagioni et al 2017).

Like everything else that's organic, burnout evolves too. The pandemic ushered in a new, more specialised type of burnout that became known as 'Zoom fatigue', initiated by the necessity of spending many hours in video conference meetings. This level of colleague interaction stretches cognitive bandwidth in novel ways. It demands more mental energy than in-person contacts due to the 'bleaching' of visual cues and the hyper-awareness level required to focus on minimised faces on our screens. While doing this, we're also effectively checking ourselves 'in the mirror', making sure we're presenting ourselves in the way we want to. This has left our Stone Age brains reeling from the assault.

It takes a while for stress to become chronic but when it does, burnout can follow quite rapidly. By contrast, recovering from burnout can take months and always requires the identification and then moderation of the root causes. Whatever those root causes are, they need to be addressed and the individual also needs to update their internal narratives related to the creation or galvanisation of stress during the experience.

The productivity and performance cost of stress

Strategies to avoid stress-related damage to employee health and wellbeing should of course be a leadership preoccupation on their own account. Yet the cost of stress and burnout extends way beyond the significant human costs. Add to this, as we've already seen, that stress is a factor in a number of common physical and mental health problems and it's not hard to predict that the issue has measurable effects on absence and turnover, engagement and productivity. It also affects issues such as long-term physical and psychosocial disability and substance dependency. It cvcn impacts the mortality rates of a company's workforce (Fletcher 1988). The business performance costs are multifactorial. Academic leader and lawyer Sir Nigel Carrington states, 'Everyone is somewhere on the mental health spectrum so this is a business productivity issue, which should be dealt with alongside other health and safety considerations. Creating a positive environment for mental health demonstrably costs less than failing to do so.' (DWP/DHSC 2017)

Unfortunately, the many ways in which employers are paying for the lack of a 'positive environment for mental health' is so well publicised that many senior leaders are tuning them out. The numbers are so unwieldy that they catch the eye but paradoxically their size renders them invisible by seeming too big to work with. They become something we already know about – a generalisation. For example, 'If it's put in the "wellbeing box" then I don't have to think about that as it's an HR/occupational health/employee relations issue.' So many stress statistics have been published since the pandemic and so many column inches have been written about its impact on mental health that we may have learned to ignore them altogether.

Just in case you've been ignoring them, here's a quick reminder. Each year, 70 million individual workdays are lost among UK-based employees because of mental health problems. This leads to British employers collectively losing £56 billion per year in 2021, compared to around £45 billion in 2019, an increase of almost 25 per cent (Deloitte 2022, DWP/DHSC 2017). A total of 18.6 million working days were reported lost due to stress, anxiety and depression in 2021/2022 (hse.gov.uk/statistics/dayslost.htm). A Gallup survey of employee engagement and satisfaction revealed that two thirds of employees reported being 'disengaged' – a well-understood outcome of relentless pressure being experienced as stress (Little & Little 2006).

Here's the evidence that people are indeed falling out of the boat and drowning in all that white water. These statistics undeniably represent a significant hole in the GDP bucket, yet they mask the detail, which is always where the devil lurks. Depending on who's doing the research, the costs are calculated in different ways. However, the costs are nearly always categorised as either direct (ie you can see the effect on the balance sheet) or indirect (you can't count it but you know it's there).

Long-term 'stress-related' absence

Long-term absence resulting from stress is much more difficult to quantify. Chronic stress will often be a cause of other potentially more serious physical health problems, which are the ones that get recorded as the source of long-term absence rather than stress. Would your organisation record the absence of the senior manager who lost his sight and was off work for a year as stress or sight loss? This gives you an idea of how challenging it is to gain a true picture of long-term stress absence.

In most cases, employees who are absent from work because of long-term stress feel so traumatised that their internal narrative rejects the very idea of returning to the same role or even the same organisation. The real causes of their sickness absence may not be recorded because they never return. Many caught up in long-term chronic stress absences find alternative employment or, if it's on offer, take early retirement. This cycle has been particularly prevalent since the pandemic, when working from home gave people a line of sight to an alternative way of living and working. The prospect of an improved quality of life became a whispered conversation and hybrid working entered stage left as a possible 'best of both worlds' solution.

Turnover

Finally, there's the cost of replacing a staff member who has left because of work-related stress. Considering it can cost upwards of £30,000 to replace just one employee, these costs should not be overlooked. Research carried out by Oxford Economics reveals that there are two main factors behind these numbers (HRreview 2014). First, the cost of 'lost output' while a replacement employee gets up to speed. Second, the logistical cost of the recruitment and assimilation process of the new employee. It's worth noting that the £30,000 price tag does not include the value of the intellectual capital and psychological collateral that they take with them when they go. Many people who leave do so with a sizable network of contacts and informal knowledge that goes with them and the informal networks of which they were a part no longer function as effectively. With these additional factors in mind, that figure may be conservative. Interestingly, Deloitte's survey found 28 per cent of UK employees intentionally left their jobs in 2021, or were planning to leave in 2022 (with 61 per cent saying the reason is due to poor mental health). The cost of replacing 28 per cent of your workforce is likely to be considerable.

The invisible costs of stress

These are the issues that count but you can't see. They are often related to the culture that you work within, those unwritten norms, beliefs, practices, attitudes and habits that set the tone of your working environment. When this environment exudes an atmosphere of trust and respect, when colleagues are self-aware enough to communicate in effective and meaningful ways, when egos are removed as self-confidence grows, with everyone becoming genuinely interested in future possibilities and synergistic outcomes, *then* employees are more likely to make good decisions, speak up when issues loom and express how they feel as pressure builds.

This adds up to a climate of what's known as psychological safety. When employees feel psychologically safe at work, they feel protected and able to be themselves, safe from the threat of negative consequences if they speak up. This perhaps doesn't sound as if it would be all that significant, until you consider how costly it is in energy and performance terms to feel unsafe and how likely it is that feeling constantly unsafc will lead to stress. It works in the other direction too. If an employee feels even remotely stressed at work, they can't feel psychologically safe – these are mutually exclusive cognitive states.

As you've seen, businesses are losing out from reduced performance and increased stress-related sickness absence. Combine this with a lack of psychological safety and the autopilot survival instinct ramps up its surveillance for threats, filtering out and firmly placing any hint of what will keep the business at the cutting edge (those higher brain activities such as creativity and innovation) on the back seat. This is because the instinct to protect ourselves, both physically and psychologically, overrides everything else. These lost opportunity costs can be difficult to quantify as they may not be obvious at the time. However, if businesses get psychological safety right, they can stay at the cutting edge, as you'll see in Chapter 5. A situation in which employees feel unable to share their ideas, concerns and insights is an expensive loss for every stakeholder on all levels. It exacerbates all the issues in the more/less quadrants, so it's worth asking yourself the questions that follow.

Chapter 3: Big questions

- ★ If you're a **team member**: if you do experience stress, how do you feel it affects your wellbeing and performance?
- ★ If you're a **people leader**: what are the performance costs of stress in your team?
- ★ If you're a **senior leader**: given all the direct and indirect costs detailed above, what would you calculate the cost to your organisation to be right now?

Key messages

- ★ Stress is directly correlated with how you uniquely perceive a situation, including yourself and others. Perceptions come from a variety of your internal filters, including past experiences, beliefs and upbringing – and perceptions can be changed. Learning to change perceptions is important as stress negatively impacts both physical and mental health.
- ★ Chronic stress has many different associated costs such as absence costs, performance costs, direct and indirect revenue costs, as well as invisible 'opportunity' costs. However, for an individual experiencing stress, the effects can be debilitating, making everyday functioning a challenge and negatively impacting personal relationships.
- ★ Despite one in six people of working age having a mental health illness, in many companies there's still a culture of silence and discrimination that needs to be addressed. As long as such attitudes exist, the associated costs of stress will take longer to reduce.

4 Sticking plasters on a broken window

Thankfully, in the decade since the first report on the effect of the Time to Change anti-stigma campaign was published, the business community has become much more alive to the fact that poor wellbeing is expensive in both human and commercial terms (Evans-Lacko et al 2014). While there's a lot of variability in what's on offer, nearly all companies now provide something to support their employees' mental wellbeing. Now that the prevalence of poor mental health has been outed in this way, open conversations are happening a lot more and mental health is rightly seen as the big modifiable factor in the overall maintenance of employee wellbeing. Because of this, more people with mental health problems feel able to speak up about their experiences and are seeking help when they need it. Being more open about wellbeing in general, and mental health in particular, is obviously helpful. However, without a deeper appreciation of causal factors and the subtle ways in which they can combine to produce positive or negative wellbeing outcomes, all that openness is not going to be worth anything beyond the immediate relief of sharing.

To capitalise on this new openness, more focused attention is urgently needed from the most senior leaders and the people managers that report to them on which specific features of the way their company is run may be at the root of the problem. Tough but necessary conversation starters might include 'How, as a leadership team, does what we tell ourselves about the options open to us [to meet our strategic objectives] narrow the options we're prepared to look at?' Also, thinking about the white water analogy, 'To what extent does our decision making create turbulence and instability in the water? How many of our employees are drenched or in the water and drowning as a result? Is the water white because of unevenness in the riverbed [unassailable features of the markets we operate in] or might it be our doing? Could the way we structure and lead our enterprise be the real reason so many people are being negatively affected by it?' It takes a brave and insightful leader to ponder these types of questions and get beyond the default response, 'Yes, but it's just the way it is.' It's not surprising therefore that so few people ask them out loud and in the company of their peers or superiors.

Who should be doing the asking?

Leaders who are curious about the roots of poor wellbeing and by extension the origins of employee engagement and organisational satisfaction undoubtedly benefit from more productive, content and engaged workforces. However, getting curious in a practical way means looking beyond the collective knowns and initiating discovery of what might be lurking below the company waterline. Senior leaders are clearly the people for this job, having the necessary circle of influence to initiate both the investigation and strategic remediation into causal factors, should they be identified. However, despite being best placed to do this, unsurprisingly (because of the fear about what they might find) this is rarely where such an investigation starts – if it starts at all. The stakeholder groups most often found 'in charge' of wellbeing are usually several rungs lower on the seniority and board influence ladder. More often than not responsibility for employee wellbeing rests with the occupational health, safety, health and environment teams or the human resources department.

On one level this makes sense. These are the business areas where employees can expect confidentiality and therefore people feel relatively safe to share their concerns and experiences. They are therefore the functions with the greatest amount of first-hand experience regarding wellbeing outcomes. They get the footfall from those who need help and are therefore in the best place to know what kind of support might be helpful. This is great for providing the support but, as this group often says, they have no influence when it comes to moving the dial on the sources of the stress that employees show up with. Their circle of concern is wider than their narrow circle of influence, meaning they're restricted to sourcing either emotional support services or personal development interventions such as resilience training.

Despite overwhelming evidence that investment in addressing the primary sources of poor wellbeing at work pays for itself many times over, only a small number of companies are directing investment towards wellbeing. Stress and poor mental health statistics tell us that people feel they have to respond to relentless work demands and it's burning them out. Rather than investigating those demands and moderating risk of damage by working directly on the sources of that pressure, employees are being sold the idea that they need to avoid damage by taking more personal responsibility for their wellbeing. The relevant services are then offered almost as a commodity solution.

Wellbeing as a commodity solution

A dizzying array of wellbeing services is being offered to employees to help them take more personal responsibility in this regard. To appreciate just how popular the commodity solution approach is, you only have to look at the growth of the wellbeing industry in the past several years. There's nothing like demand to stimulate supply and the global wellbeing industry hasn't disappointed in the provision of smart and scalable interventions to salve and support the stressed employee.

The global stress management treatments market was estimated at $17.2 billion in 2019 and is forecast to reach $20.6 billion by 2024, a compound annual growth rate of 3.7 per cent for the forecast period (Javed 2020). Taking wellbeing interventions as a totality, the market is worth $1.5 trillion (Callaghan et al 2021). Predictably, with so many services available to buy into, wellbeing strategies contain offerings as diverse and varied as:

- ★ employee helplines
- ★ peripatetic or permanent occupational health (OH) support
- ★ health and lifestyle education and promotion
- ★ life coaching and personal health and wellbeing consultancy
- ★ nutrition advice
- ★ sleep clinics
- ★ subsidised gym memberships
- ★ free fruit in the office
- ★ onsite counselling
- ★ mental health first aid
- ★ mindfulness and free apps
- ★ lunchtime yoga
- ★ group exercise and running clubs
- ★ personal resilience development
- ★ support with women's health issues
- ★ menopause support

... and so on. The list is long.

Taken singly or in combination, these interventions do have real worth and many have the potential to support an individual with their mental health and wellbeing. Helping employees to be more aware and responsible for their own wellbeing is sensible but this should be a strand in a wider strategy rather than the strategy itself. In a rather ironic twist, the message that 'We want to help you protect your own wellbeing and to help you do that we have provided lots of wonderful support services for you to use' often adds an additional layer of pressure. Many of the people we help tell us that they feel guilty about not being able to find the time to access the support that's provided for them. Given that they're often already feeling overwhelmed, it's a short and common cognitive hop from here to 'So really, it's my fault that I feel like this'. Remember how the brain generalises and is biased to seek confirmation. This ironic twist could actually be compounding the issue.

Many of the people we see at this stage are genuinely struggling to cope and as a result their performance is often declining. It can therefore be helpful to have access to confidential support. Ironically, when a wellbeing service is 'popular' the organisation is rightly pleased it's being used, thus demonstrating that the decision to invest in the service was a good one. Basking in the warm glow of rewarded good intention, conversations are then had about how to extend or augment the service in some way so that others may be similarly supported. This is great but only up to a point. Life is full of surprises and people will need support from time to time as unanticipated events or storms rear up. But this type of support only goes so far and may only provide temporary relief. Little research has been done longitudinally on the effects of long-term benefits from resilience training. Our own unpublished research shows that these effects do wear off quite quickly, usually around three to six months post training. The unanswered question is: why is the service so popular in the first place? The way we see it, the proliferation of wellbeing services in some companies does seem to correlate with a sort of wilful myopia to which the corrective prescription is always a further extension of wellbeing services.

With so many solutions available, wellbeing has become a commodity. The same economic system that creates the conditions for poor wellbeing has also commoditised mental health and wellbeing solutions into products and services that can be bought into for profit. There's a distressing circularity to this that's highly visible in the relatively new concept of wellness sabbaticals. The idea here is that, for a week, the employer grants the employee permission to focus on their wellbeing, perhaps to leave work on time or take a yoga class or two. The purpose of the exercise is to create and legitimise space to recharge and recover through active engagement with the other interests in their life. That this special opportunity is often positioned as an employee benefit, almost an act of employer philanthropy, speaks volumes about three rather alarming things. The first is just how normalised the potential for employee burnout has become if, in order to stave it off, you need to schedule some focused self-care. The second is how inflated employer expectations of their employees have become if even the employer feels a wellness sabbatical might be a good idea. And the third, perhaps the most worrisome, is that having created the conditions that risk burnout it's the employer who grants the employee a five-day window of opportunity to try and correct the imbalance.

Most of the wellbeing services we see in our consulting work do contribute something. If they could be made to integrate more effectively with each other then they might also deliver something valuable to a broader wellbeing strategy. Every wellbeing investment is well intentioned. However, the thread that runs through all the most popular interventions is that they're either focused on 'repair' to a damaged individual or are designed to help minimise negative wellbeing impacts by building personal resilience. People who use the services are grateful but the money invested does nothing to uncover and address what's driving people to need these services in the first place. These types of intervention are just sticking plasters on broken windows.

The services are popular because even the most enlightened senior leaders don't know enough about the current level of mental wellbeing in their workplace or how company-specific factors are amplifying or moderating it. Their lack of understanding about this dynamic is a weakness as deteriorating mental health in the workplace, even if the workplace itself is not the only causal factor, is a significant business risk and a threat to business reliability. Conversely, higher levels of employee wellbeing facilitate an invaluable competitive advantage in terms of attendance, retention, full engagement, creativity, adaptability and, critically, ability to innovate. This is the reason why so many research-based companies such as GlaxoSmithKline, Pfizer and AstraZeneca invested in employee wellbeing and performance programmes many years before other industries. When we started our business, these were the types of companies we worked with most of the time; they knew that pressure was a catalyst for growth and discovery but only up to a point. Stress is the enemy of experimentation and innovation, both of which are the discovery lifeblood of their industry.

Managing risk three ways

Most other business risks are dealt with by using a combination of intervention approaches. The first of these, the primary interventions, are designed to limit loss via targeted prevention. Secondary interventions are aimed at moderating the impact of risk factors – in other words loss reduction; and tertiary interventions are designed to offer fast remediation. Most risk management follows this format and physical occupational health risks are certainly approached in this way.

To keep it simple, let's use the example of a rotating blade in a production process. A physical hazard is clearly present and represents a visible risk to an operator. A primary intervention would be to remove it from the process altogether but if there's no other way to cut that component your next step will be to place it under a guard and therefore make it as safe as you can. This is a secondary intervention, which will dramatically lower the risk of injury. However, despite this intervention a small risk remains. The blade guard is necessarily made of metal and our operative has soft hands. A scratch now and again is a possibility so you have an accident book and a nurse with a first aid box ready to offer a plaster if required. The sticking plaster would be a tertiary intervention.

If it works this way for physical health risks, why are leaders so reluctant to apply the same methodology to psychosocial health risks, particularly when we know that mounting work pressure combined with a reduced ability to balance that with renewal is acting in the same way as the rotating knife?

The management standards and guidance for the management of workplace psychosocial health risks issued by the Health and Safety Executive make it clear that primary prevention is best practice and that the blend of all three levels of intervention detailed in Figure 1 below is needed. Despite the obvious logic of this approach and strong encouragement from the HSE, investigation into the sources of workplace pressure is still a rare occurrence in most companies. Interventions mostly fall into the secondary and tertiary categories. They're paid for by the company but the emphasis is on the employee managing the risk of stress and burnout by developing more resilience (the blade guard in the example above) or the employer helping them recover once their mental wellbeing has been affected (the sticking plaster from the nurse). There's no balancing investigation into whether the blade is necessary, how sharp it is or how fast it's spinning.

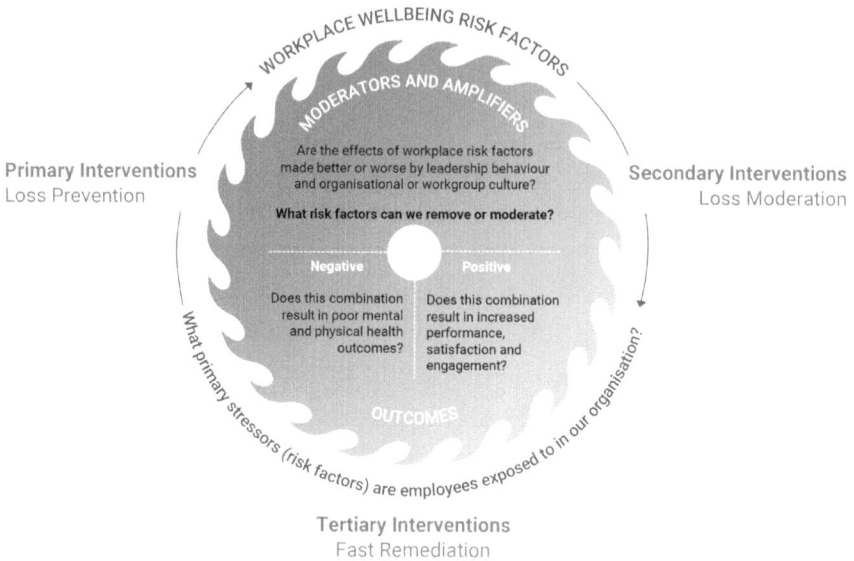

Figure 1: The three levels of intervention

Where's the smoking gun?

Few leaders seem interested in exploring what specific and modifiable workplace factors might be behind the wellbeing issues in their business and using this information to take a more primary prevention approach to improve it. There seem to be three codependent reasons why this activity is missing from most wellbeing strategies. The first of these is mutual and self-sustaining acceptance among many senior leadership teams that the way the business is currently resourced and managed is the only option that exists. 'Competitive pressure brings constraints so there's little point in tinkering or uncovering issues we can't fix.' So goes the narrative.

This belief is supported by a second linked conviction that spare employee capacity remains in the system. The metaphorical Covey jar (see appleseeds.org/Big-Rocks_Covey.htm and Covey nd), already acknowledged to be brimful of big rocks, smaller rocks, pebbles, sand and most recently the water, still has space for 25cl more contribution. The stress and mental health statistics provide a clear indication that this notion is more hopeful than it is accurate. The sides of that jar are already wet and those out there at the sharp end (who do not share this delusion) have lived experience of this fact.

The third reason has its roots in the inertia created by the first two ideas in that senior leaders are often not clear about where to look for explanations and they don't like to admit that. This is to be expected. Workplace dynamics are complex and the variables are as numerous and different from each other as the people who operate within them. But treating a glancing graze from a sniper bullet before taking a good look at the rooftops or attempting to locate the smoke as a clue to the whereabouts of the gun risks a potentially fatal second shot. The number of people absent from work, the footfall to emotional support services and the employee assistance programme (EAP) engagement reports all provide useful metrics on the volume of casualties. However, they provide scant information about the nature or location of the weapons that actually caused the wounds.

If I don't ask, I won't get (what I don't want to deal with)

The failure to look into the underlying sources of poor workplace wellbeing is not therefore an oversight. Over the past 20 or so years, if our work has taught us anything it's that, like so much of what does and doesn't get said at work, the decision not to ask the uncomfortable questions is rooted in fear:

- ★ fear of uncovering issues that are believed to be insoluble
- ★ fear of being held personally responsible for opening a

Pandora's box without a means to catch what escapes
★ fear of negative consequences because you started something you couldn't finish on your own and it looks as if nobody is coming with you.

This anxiety is predictable and easy to relate to. As someone once said to us, 'I'm reluctant to spend a shed load of money asking questions to uncover a problem I've got to spend a shedload of money fixing.' Even we agree this doesn't sound all that appealing. While the fear of this unknown is undoubtedly real, the reality of discovery is much less frightening than you might imagine. The sceptic in question was visualising an investigative process that took the form of a classic top-down, company-wide survey with all the associated difficulties of local leadership action planning, engagement with potentially unpopular results and consultant-heavy meetings and recommendations. Looking for a smoking gun or finding better ways to meet work challenges doesn't have to be so difficult or miserable. There are many effective and enjoyable ways to tap into the priceless insight rattling around inside your employees.

In a world where competition for resources and markets is becoming more and more intense, leaders at all levels are going to need that line of sight on what drives *good* wellbeing in their organisation. So far we've focused on understanding what causes poor wellbeing and, yes, there's an urgent requirement for a more focused approach to these factors. But it's important not to lose sight of the fact that while you're uncovering the stuff that gets in the way, you'll also discover more about what enhances employee wellbeing and learn about the conditions under which employees are their most creative, productive, collaborative and so on. Apart from being a much more emotionally and intellectually appealing activity, looking below the surface gives you all the information you need to simultaneously reduce wellbeing losses for those affected and further enhance wellbeing for those who are not yet negatively affected. It's the equivalent of moving everyone a few stages to the right towards 'fulfilment' on the mental wellbeing continuum we introduced in Chapter 3.

The data you'll need to do this is already in your organisation – it's freely available, in real time, and it automatically refreshes every day. It's permanently backed up and you don't need any special tools or skills to capture it. Even more importantly, if your people go to work for your competitors, it's potentially priceless, as they take the data with them. This data usually stays in the minds of the individuals, because nobody asks for it. Hundreds of hours of running focus groups have told us that even if employee insight is sought, most people doubt it's safe to say what they really think so don't say anything or conclude that there's no point risking it because nothing will change anyway.

The mosquito in the room

All levels of leadership will benefit from listening to what employees are desperate to tell them but to access these benefits they need to get over their fear of hearing it. Those leaders that are brave enough to ask the right questions and get curious about the perspectives of their employees generally hear different things from those they expected. This is backed up by our own research. When we help leaders and managers facilitate this type of discussion we see repeatedly that what people want to talk about are not complex issues that are difficult and expensive to fix but smaller things that are more achievable. Just because a change is modest doesn't mean it won't be effective. If they're in the right place and alleviate an uncomfortable source of pressure for an individual, they'll have a positive wellbeing and performance impact. As the late Anita Roddick, former CEO of Body Shop, once said, 'If you think you are too small to have an impact, try sleeping with a mosquito in the room.' Modern workplaces are full of metaphorical mosquitos – small annoyances and irritants that have the potential to puncture the skin, raise a welt and lead to more serious disease. Employees know where they hatch as well as how to possibly get rid of them. If you're open enough to ask, some of your people will tell you. If you want more than a few to share their insights with you then the cultural conditions will of course have to be right. How to lay the foundation stones for a culture that will create these conditions is the subject of the next chapter. You may be pleased to learn that the price of these foundation stones runs on a rate card from very inexpensive to totally free.

If, like us, you've spent time listening to employees describe their experiences at work, what you'll discover is that under the surface layers of negativity and stress, the loudest message is about powerlessness. Interwoven with all the day to day detail is what they're really struggling with, which often is not the details of the day job but a lack of agency, a sense of having no voice and therefore no meaningful opportunity for influence. This can develop for a number of reasons. Like many other sources of workplace stress, it's most commonly rooted in fear and related issues around lack of trust and respect, feeling excluded, lack of confidence and low-grade anxieties about the negative consequences of using any voice they feel they do have.

This fits with what we know. As detailed in Figure 1 and the more/less quadrant in Chapter 2, external factors combine to generate employee pressures but it's the amplifying or moderating effect of other factors that shape the effect that pressure has on wellbeing and performance. Pressure in itself is neutral and isn't a problem if equalised by the correct response habits and strategies. Indeed, the saying that 'good work is good for you' is acknowledged to be the truth (Waddell & Burton 2006). However the default assumption made by most leaders that the work in their organisation is both *automatically* and *universally* good is potentially a problem. How do they know? What evidence is taken as proof that the assumption is correct? Evidence from the statistics on mental health in the workplace and the attrition rate post pandemic suggests the assumption is problematic. As evidence of this, look no further than the 2023 UK nurses strike, the first ever national strike action following years of understaffing, escalating workloads and declining standards, leaving nurses feeling powerless to provide care and support in the way they feel they need to, as well as being thoroughly demoralised.

Even if at one time the 'work here is good' assumption was correct, does it necessarily follow that it's still true? The pandemic years irrevocably changed the world of work and the people in it. How does the work feel now? Who's loving hybrid working? Who loves it a bit less and why? What are the major sources of pressure for the team now? What makes them worse? What makes them feel better? What one modifiable factor would make the biggest difference to the greatest number of people on the team? What do we need to do to make it happen?

Most companies conduct an employee satisfaction or engagement survey at least once a year but these top-down approaches won't provide you with sufficiently granular detail to influence the working lives of individuals who are struggling. Surveys such as these are useful and can illuminate common themes but, as we've said, the really valuable stuff is in the contextual detail. A more sources-based approach to wellbeing strategy development, based on the insight of the people whose wellbeing the strategy exists to protect, would provide valuable answers to these important questions.

Best practice

As would be expected, the HSE is unequivocal about the need for primary prevention (see hse.gov.uk/stress/standards), built upon regular assessment of stress risk factors such as work demands, extent and frequency of organisational change, lack of control and influence, role clarity, working relationships and support and training. The work we do with our own clients follows this model with the addition of exploration of organisational culture.

Most leaders report that gaining this type of granular insight into the way their team experiences the pressures detailed in Figure 2 is extremely valuable. This was ever the case with global or decentralised teams but now that day to day in-person contact has become less frequent as a result of hybrid working, these insights are felt to be even more revealing. Those that use the approach concur that a 'map' of where people feel the pressure comes from, how they respond to it and what impact this has on their energy helps them focus team development time in the most beneficial places. This speeds up conversations about what gets in the way of performance as well as what degrades energy and wellbeing. It builds trust and encourages experimentation with new approaches that are perhaps more suited to how we live and work. In essence they're able to have safe and constructive dialogue about how to do more with the same or less without getting damaged in the process. Knowing where possible incremental health and performance gains might exist obviously increases the chances that you'll find some. This is all common sense but is surprisingly uncommon as an approach. Why is this?

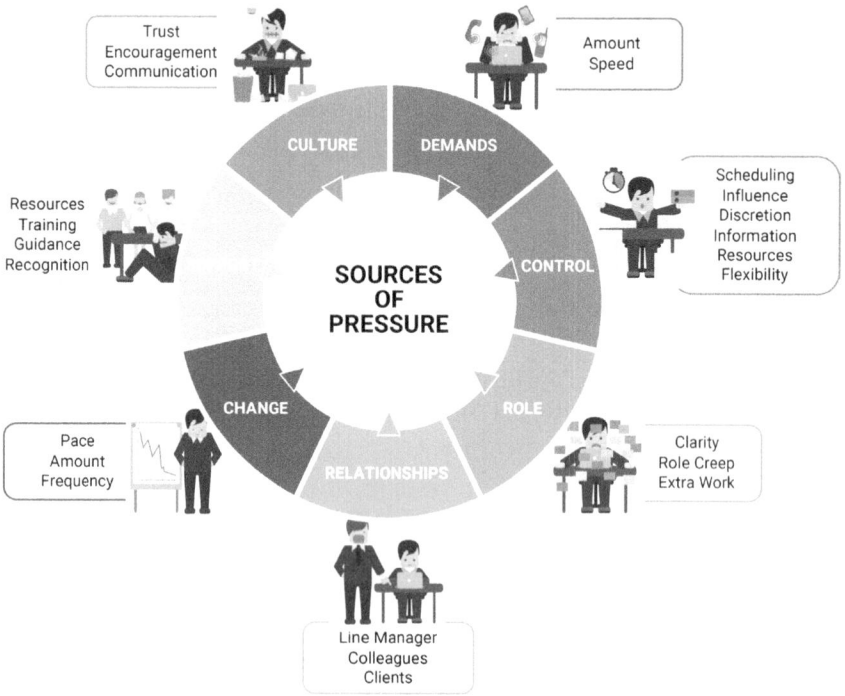

Figure 2: Sources of workplace pressure

We run several types of leadership development workshops, among them one specifically designed to help delegates create greater team resilience. The focus of their training is to be better catalysts for latent creativity and contribution in their teams. This obviously involves them looking at how they behave but also requires them to know where their team is starting from in relation to the healthy high-performance behaviours they hope to encourage. To help them do this, as part of the pre-work, all are offered the option to gather this information prior to the session. They have up to three weeks to do this. All that's asked of them is to supply the email addresses of their team members so that we can administer the assessment to each of them and send the manager (and only the manager, by the way) the 'map' of where the team are now. This covers key areas such as fatigue, recovery, perception of pressure and how psychologically safe they feel within the team. This is offered as part of the training so they can see the world through their team's eyes and use this knowledge to work *with* that insight, rather than against it.

The team profile that they receive will be of obvious benefit to them during their own training but it will also provide an invaluable baseline against which to assess team development. Despite there being no cost barrier to obtaining this team report, *less than half of attendees arrive at the session with their team's data.* When asked why they didn't take up the opportunity they usually say something to the effect that 'It didn't seem necessary because I know my team really well' (or a variant of the same idea). While this may sound reasonable, what they're unfortunately left with is having to navigate their way through their own skills development session with a generalised view of what's going on for the team right now. We imagine that these same managers wouldn't dream of going to a finance meeting without their budget spreadsheet, yet where human resource leadership is concerned, it seems that a general sense of how people are doing is considered to be enough.

Here's another old narrative playing out – that you don't really need this type of information as you've managed perfectly well up to now without it. But here's the thing: the world has changed. Whatever worked before now isn't guaranteed to work as well in the future. The rapid increase in cases of work-related stress already tells you that the way you're working is not working as well as it did. Knowing what you (think) you know won't necessarily get you where you need to go. Hybrid working has introduced completely new challenges and removed a lot of day to day contact with colleagues which, for many, provided limitless opportunities for personal development, knowledge sharing, ideation and exploration and basic relationship building. Many of the leaders and managers we work with still seem to assume a kind of universal employee experience. However, the endless distorting, deleting and generalisation performed by human brains means that every workday experience is, by definition, unique to each team member. With the pace of life so fast and with so many competing claims on employees' time and attention, it's no longer enough to simply guess how 'good' the work is. All levels of leadership must be prepared to create safe spaces for the people who report to them so that they can speak up, share their insights and receive feedback, even if the feedback isn't what they want to hear. All parties need to get more comfortable with initiating and participating in potentially uncomfortable conversations and to capture the resulting information without judgement in a format that can be collectively worked on. The hardest step is the first one – deciding to include investigation in the wellbeing strategy. Engaging staff and harvesting insight is relatively easy once you've decided to be bold and 'risk' it. There are plenty of tools to help managers and leaders gather what they need to know and assimilate it in a way that simplifies local action planning around it.

To manage the risk of people having poor mental health, it is essential to gain insight into:

* how people feel about their workload
* how change is managed
* how much control and influence they feel have
* how clear they are about their role
* the quality of their working relationships
* how safe they feel being themselves and sharing their experience.

You don't have to agree with it and you quite possibly won't but that doesn't matter. It's a window on what looks better to them and in wellbeing and performance terms, particularly with highly engaged teams, better for them leads to better for you too.

Towards more open workplace cultures

There's no easy way to measure organisational culture because there are so many factors that combine to create it. It's interesting to note that not long after the HSE published its stress risk management standards the requirement to measure organisational culture was quickly dropped on the grounds that it wasn't possible to achieve a reliable measure for it in the assessment tool. That it was initially included demonstrates central government recognition of the role that organisational culture plays in dialling pressure either up or down. These are all big factors in wellbeing outcomes:

- ★ understanding how people experience their workday, with specific reference to how safe people feel to speak up if they're struggling
- ★ whether they feel it's safe to be themselves (or whether they have to wear a kind of work mask)
- ★ how much trust they have towards their leadership and their colleagues.

In addition to staff satisfaction and employee engagement surveys, many large companies also conduct specific culture surveys, which is great, if a bit odd. Doing it this way appears to treat it as somehow separate from other factors, like an ingredient in the company soup. But the culture of an organisation is the stock in which the other ingredients float and, as all cooks know, the quality of the broth very much affects the flavour of the soup! The culture of the company can be 'read' by the way people answer more specific questions around workplace pressure, how close people feel to burnout or how safe people feel to speak up about the factors that are influencing their health and wellbeing. These are specific topics and the questions in many culture surveys just feel a bit general. Unsurprisingly, what comes out of this type of survey is fairly general too which, like the employee satisfaction and engagement assessments, makes the data hard to act on. Maybe they've grown in popularity because their generalised nature makes them feel safe to carry out?

However, safety works in two directions at once. Unless employees feel that the culture of the company they work for openly celebrates honesty – that is to say the people who work there are 100 per cent confident that honesty is really what's wanted and there won't be any negative consequences from being honest – then few will be prepared to take the interpersonal risk required to say what they really feel or share what they know. They save that for friends, partners and therapists – which, by the way, is how we know what it is they'd share if they believed it was safe to do so.

Truth or vital lie?

The fact that so many employees don't feel it's safe to be honest about the difficulties they may be having in meeting deadlines or squaring conflict between their personal purpose and company demands, or any other negative impact that work might be having on them, is a major threat to wellbeing and performance sustainability. When people tell you nothing or only what they think you want to hear, you're in trouble. If you aren't asking the questions or you are and this is all you're getting from people, then the only wellbeing strategy open to you is stockpiling wellbeing remediation and hoping for the best. This therefore goes some way to explaining the proliferation of wellbeing strategies built around tertiary intervention.

Initiating primary prevention through the identification and moderation of root causes means you need to create a culture where people feel sufficiently psychologically safe to be honest. When people don't fear a negative outcome from sharing what they feel or know, then the barrier is raised, exposing new perspectives, valuable experience, novel insights and fresh ideas. There's little downside to experimentation in environments where failure is seen as a personal or team 'little learn' and a step towards fast-tracked workgroup and organisational development. Making it possible for people to share the data of their lived experience makes the company boat move faster, upright and in the right direction. At the same time it offers a significant, zero-cost opportunity to dramatically increase employee satisfaction, engagement and productivity while also enhancing wellbeing and performance sustainability.

You have to wonder why more companies haven't done it.

Chapter 4: Big questions

- ★ If you're a **team member**: how open are you with colleagues and managers about the impact that work demands are having on other aspects of your life?
- ★ If you're a **people leader**: do you have a measure of how good the work actually is for your team or are you making assumptions?
- ★ If you're a **senior leader**: if you were asked, would you be able to describe the top three systemic issues facing your organisation in terms of employee and performance sustainability?

Key messages

- ★ Greater awareness is needed regarding the real sources of pressure and poor workplace wellbeing.
- ★ Everyone is a stakeholder and has separate but conjoined responsibilities to address the issues at source.
- ★ Employees know better than senior leaders where the low-hanging fruit is to be found.
- ★ To get at this insight, workplace cultures need to be psychologically safe.

𝒴5 Towards greater psychological safety

The question is, how do companies go about creating a more open, candid culture? How is it possible to make employees feel psychologically safer to speak up and share their insights? Psychological safety was first defined in the 1960s and has more recently been made popular by Harvard Business School psychologist Amy Edmondson (Schein & Bennis 1965; Edmondson 2019). At an individual and team level, the current definition of psychological safety is aligned with the sense of feeling safe to voice ideas, seek and provide feedback, collaborate with others and experiment with new ways of working. People must also feel able to take a wider assessment of what Amy Edmondson refers to in her work as 'interpersonal risks' when collaborating with teammates and leaders.

As David Altman, the COO of the Center for Creative Leadership, points out, 'Psychological safety at work doesn't mean everybody is nice all the time. It means that you embrace the conflict and speak up, knowing that your team has your back.' (Altman nd) At an organisational level it can be defined as the formal and informal practices and procedures that guide and support open and trustworthy interactions at work, creating an environment in which employees are able to speak up without fear of being rejected or punished.

What matters most for our purposes is that when people feel psychologically safe they're able to share knowledge and information about tackling the root causes of wellbeing issues. They can also propose new ideas for organisational improvement or take the initiative to develop new products or ways of working without fear of recrimination, censorship, ridicule or being penalised. It's the ability, according to Google's Matt Sakaguchi, to take off the work mask and talk about the messy or the sad, to have difficult conversations with colleagues and to focus on collaborating with other teams instead of just focusing on efficiency (Duhigg 2016). Unsurprisingly, high levels of psychological safety have been shown to have a positive impact on employee productivity, aiding team and organisational learning, growth, contribution and performance sustainability.

To appreciate how beneficial improved psychological safety can be in the recalibration of our workplaces, a wider perspective is needed. Relentless pressure to perform inevitably narrows focus to the task in preference to the humans actually performing the task. Quick fixes get favoured over slower burn developments and, against a backdrop of global recovery from the pandemic and subsequent economic crises facing many countries, governments and organisations increasingly turn to innovation to shore up sustainability. Of particular interest to policymakers are those innovations linked to production processes, work organisation and human resource management practices. These are the innovations considered most likely to bring about competitive advantage for an organisation. Many companies pursue them yet the results are disappointing. The major factors in this lack of success are likely to be the absence of critical complementary contingencies such as a supportive organisational climate and a collaborative working environment.

To achieve collaboration, the working environment needs to be one where employees genuinely value each other's contributions to work processes and don't just listen politely before championing their own cause. They need to feel safe enough to take those interpersonal risks. They also need to be brave enough to say something that might attract a negative response. Even though they may not label it as such, people need to feel they're operating in a climate of psychological safety. When people do feel safe, they give their employer and colleagues their discretionary effort – time, energy and outputs willingly given for free – and commercially invaluable insights. They do this because they feel personally valued, comfortable that their contribution is held in high esteem because they are, as a consequence, emotionally and intellectually engaged in what they're doing.

The Pixar Animation Studios story

Organisations that have made the investment in fostering a strong climate of psychological safety tend to outperform those that haven't, as compelling case studies demonstrate. In fact, some studies have shown that psychological safety is the single strongest influence on performance (Duhigg 2016). Google's Aristotle research project claims that, more than anything else, psychological safety is critical to making a team work. This can clearly be seen at Pixar Animation Studios, where the co-founder and long-term CEO Ed Catmull works tirelessly and intentionally to create and maintain a climate of psychological safety. He understands that to reach magnificence, you must push back to get through the boring, sappy and mediocre while not taking the pushback personally but seeing it as part of the journey to outstanding results.

Catmull deliberately creates a structural approach to improve employees' morale and pride in their work. He does this, according to Edmondson, by establishing meetings and review sessions for the purpose of generating candid feedback. He did away with a rigid chain of command structure to explicitly enforce free-flowing communication between all positions within the company, thereby discouraging isolation. He also prioritised workers' wellbeing, enabling retention of the highest calibre people and ensuring the company's sustainability. In addition to these structural changes, he ensured there were also behavioural changes that promoted psychological safety. He uses techniques such as admitting his own fallibility by sharing his own mistakes. He presents a persona of humility to his staff and shows a genuine interest in them. He's curious about what they're doing and how they're approaching things.

Because of the strong interpersonal nature of psychological safety, getting it right can be a balancing act. According to Julia Rozovsky, Google's Project Aristotle researcher, it can be messy and difficult (Duhigg 2016). This is because psychological safety can be breached, violated and damaged. Therefore anyone interested in maximising human capital in the workplace needs to understand under which circumstances the damage occurred and, importantly, how that damage might be repaired. As an example, think about trust, a prerequisite to psychological safety. Trust acts as a partial mediator between 'input variables' such as leadership, organisational culture and team characteristics and 'output variables' such as performance, learning and innovation. If trust is lost for an employee, it would be useful for a manager to understand why and how the trust was lost and how it has impacted the employee's perception of their personal psychological safety so that it can be repaired. If the employee loses trust because a colleague has ridiculed their idea, for example, or has criticised their attempts to learn and collaborate they're unlikely to contribute their ideas again, even if those ideas could be highly beneficial to the organisation. That criticism or ridicule can leave them feeling negatively judged, stupid and shamed. If an employee is continually negatively judged, this may impact their mental health along with their ability to disclose their feelings or access mental health services and support. By understanding the circumstances under which trust and ultimately psychological safety are damaged, the manager has the knowledge to intercede. They can then proactively drive an agenda for the whole team to value each other's contributions, be respectful in their challenge and feedback to each other and to develop curiosity about the possibilities put forward by their colleagues.

Employees who feel they work in an environment fraught with conflict, retribution, fear of getting it wrong or upsetting someone – especially environments advocating strict hierarchy – are much less likely to admit to their mistakes. This represents an additional loss to the organisation, over and above the economic cost of the error, because if mistakes are hidden, neither individuals, teams nor the wider organisation are able to learn and grow from them. It may sound contradictory but having a higher error reporting rate is not a negative thing, as one of Edmonson's studies found (1996). She discovered that higher levels of psychological safety in hospitals were associated with higher rates of drug error reporting. The ability to routinely report mistakes enabled the hospital to develop preventative strategies such as double-checking each other's work to optimise patient safety. However, working in an environment where psychological safety is low means people are more likely to focus energy and effort on minimising risk, self-preservation and keeping their head down for fear of it being bitten off should they dare to lift it above the parapet. You need only look at the infamous Wells Fargo story to understand how such corporate disasters make it possible to trace the origins of dangerous or expensive decision making back to a lack of psychological safety. Such was the lack of that safety that for years employees were too afraid to push back on the unattainable targets forced upon them, opting instead to cross unethical and eventually criminal boundaries in the pursuit of target achievement. The result was Wells Fargo being fined nearly $3.7 billion for illegal practices, misapplied payments, wrongful foreclosures, and incorrect fees and interest charges.

Team dysfunction

One of our own research participants highlighted the dysfunctional aspects of teams when psychological safety is low. She said that her organisation strove to create a competitive environment where everyone fought to be on top, to shine their own light, following the mantra that if one person improves, everyone improves. However, poor execution of this modus operandi led to insecurities and a lack of trust between team members. As a result, instead of improving performance, everything slowed down. The lack of trust spawned tortuously long decision-making processes, suspicion around the hidden roots of decisions when they were made and a lack of confidence to rely on others. Far from increasing collaboration it created single-track workers. There was an unwillingness to 'grab the whole project' and instead individuals looked after their own 'swim lanes', always making sure they were marginally ahead of others, to 'dodge the bullet'. Energy was 'horrible', team members kept things to themselves, refused to share information, tripped others up in meetings and developed 'nasty work practices'. The team was 'fragmented and cutthroat – one colleague suffered severe mental health issues and was on the verge of breakdown'. Another claimed that five out of seven team members were leaving the organisation he worked in because they didn't feel psychologically safe with their leader. They didn't feel heard – they were talked over in meetings, their contribution wasn't recognised, they didn't have clear targets, nor were their opinions valued. Ultimately many became ill prior to leaving the organisation.

The team and the whole self

In marked contrast to the outcomes from these examples, our own research confirms that when psychological safety is high, people show up to work with their whole self. This allows different points of view to be shared, individual perspectives to be explored and opinions to be freely aired. Because psychological safety is inclusive, any behaviour or response that's felt to be personally injurious can be called out at that moment before the individual retreats cognitively, emotionally or both and effectively seals themselves off from the group. People can say *how* something has landed for them, helping others see alternative perspectives and grow from this knowledge.

Such interpersonal behaviour is great for relationships and personal wellbeing, reducing the potential for inadvertent negativity and threat. Just as importantly, from a performance perspective it also creates a vested interest in the organisation and what it's doing. People become motivated to succeed for the greater good – not just for personal gain. Under these conditions people are also able to work smarter through their ability to be open about underperformance in an encouraging way. Causal factors can then be broken down, explored and supported. This develops trust and one way to tell if trust exists in a team is to look at the amount of fun the members have and how happy they are. Another of our research participants put it very well: 'Team members speak up, challenge, give each other a hard time – with good intentions. The energy is much higher than in other teams. Instead of dreading meetings, people look forward to seeing each other, generating even more energy. There's an undercurrent of individual commitment to the team and for team success.'

It's clear that this type of culture results in people being better able to cope with pressure and being more motivated. They feel more valued and respected, and are able to live by a strong value set. As we saw in the first chapter, conflict between personal and organisational values can be expensively disruptive to both wellbeing and performance. The cliche 'our employees are our most important asset' is heard less often now but most companies say they still feel it to be the case. Yet for an organisation to really value its people, it also needs to look closely at its own set of values and assess the extent to which macro and micro decision making embodies and supports those stated values. It's easy to say one thing but do something quite different. We see plenty of examples of just that in our work.

A company we work with provided a recent example of how easy it is to espouse one set of values and really believe in them yet unintentionally behave in a highly non-congruent way. They have a strong drive to develop world-class leaders, advocating that all leaders must create psychologically safe spaces for their teams. They're clear about what that culture looks like and passionate about the benefits. However, intense internal performance pressures driven by the need to remain globally competitive compels them to offer only an hour-long e-learning intervention for their leaders to learn how to do so!

Which behaviours create safety?

Creating a climate of psychological safety throughout an organisation can be messy. Annoyingly, you can't do it as a solo operation either. It requires the involvement of everyone and for all stakeholders to be accountable for their role in the development process. But it's not inherently difficult. The behaviours involved are intuitive and sensible and psychological safety grows organically when these learnable behaviours accumulate among leaders and their team members.

To help anchor these behaviours in an easily digestible form, we've combined the most recent Harvard Business School thinking with our own empirical research to create what we call the 'five Cs' model. You can use this to guide the development of psychologically safer spaces where you work. The simple model shows the interrelationship of five behavioural fundamentals, which accelerate openness and trust: peer to peer, leader to leader or line manager to team member. These five behaviours are distinct but mutually supportive. We will detail each in turn and offer tools and suggestions to help anyone bring them naturally into their leadership or, in the case of non-managers, into their interaction with others.

The five fundamentals focus on developing the confidence you need to become more curious about the unique perspectives of others, talk to the person and not the task, get more from each collaboration and further develop self-confidence and trust through the medium of this self-perpetuating cycle.

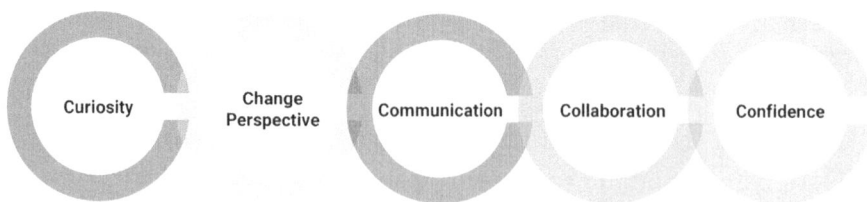

Figure 1 – The five Cs model

Curiosity

It may seem odd that curiosity is so important when it comes to creating psychological safety. However, there must be an element of curiosity for you to have read the book to this point. Human beings are naturally curious. You might be curious about what the day will bring, what the weather will be like, what your living room will look like painted a different colour, what your next car will be. What often happens, however, is the pressure of day to day living and working dampens your natural curiosity, sometimes to the point where you close off opportunities or the ability to see things from alternative perspectives. Ignorance may be bliss for some but that bliss is likely to be short lived as the world rapidly changes around you.

By extending natural curiosity into the world of work, you can give yourself a great opportunity for understanding at a deeper level. You can become a wiser human being who's less likely to fly off the handle at the next little thing that triggers you. You can develop the ability not to take every little thing personally. As we've seen, when you're feeling overwhelmed or stuck in a negative emotional dip you're more vulnerable and susceptible to taking things personally that aren't aimed at you. In turn this will push you to respond emotionally – from the chimp brain, as Steve Peters says (2013). Developing a wider sense of curiosity will enable you to continually ask yourself what's beyond this, or what the reasons are behind this happening.

Without such questions you'll continue to hold on to existing views or judgements, responding accordingly. This may result in you becoming passive in the way you live and work, or it may mean you'll miss new ideas, opportunities and possibilities. It will also make it more likely that you'll stay stuck in your current story because you won't uncover anything that will challenge it. Curiosity helps to break up the mundane and routine as you constantly pay attention to the world around you, questioning it, looking at it in new ways. Challenge yourself to get curious about why people do certain things or respond in certain ways. Get curious about why decisions have been made at work or why there are particular ways of doing things. Get curious about other teams – learn more about what they do, why they do things the way they do and how they like to work.

One important factor evident in current thinking around psychological safety and one that has come through strongly in our own research is the ability to be inclusive. This relates not just to those who may have different personality traits from you but also to those who may have different beliefs, come from different cultures or find themselves living and working in a different culture from the one they were brought up in. As one of our research participants said, 'Be open to cultural differences, challenge your internal perceptions about what is and isn't allowed, be open, flexible and adaptable to the circumstances you find yourself in.' Become curious about what's considered respectful expression of cultural differences. This can be tricky to navigate, especially if, for example, culturally you've been brought up with a teacher-centred approach where you keep your thoughts to yourself and don't share information or in a risk-free environment whereby the most senior person is the only one who can initiate change. Working in an environment that requires people to develop curiosity, to be open, speak up and put forward ideas can feel uncomfortable for some, so you need to be aware of this and adapt your responses accordingly.

Such curiosity will, ultimately, make your life easier, as you develop a deeper understanding of your workplace, its culture and the people within it. It will enable you to stay out of blame and judgement or feeling internally at odds with yourself. This is crucial when developing psychological safety because as soon as you blame or negatively judge yourself, others or situations, psychological safety in that environment will have been compromised. Your negative perception will result in you unintentionally projecting your blame and judgement – through your body language and voice qualities – onto others, impacting how they in turn respond to you. One research participant explained how her line manager 'replicated what he learned from his previous organisation that he believed made it so good to work for'. He deliberately prompted his team to share their experiences as he was curious to hear their perspectives; she felt that 'he had the qualities and attributes of a line manager who's attuned to hearing difference'.

Another important area to become curious about is the unknown potential for your product, service, team or organisation. Being curious has resulted in some industries being severely disrupted. Toyota's 2019 'What If?' and Cuvva's 2016 'What if car insurance wasn't sh*t?' campaigns both followed Honda's 2013 'Hands – the power of dreams. Let's see what curiosity can do' campaign. All these promotions were designed to challenge car drivers to think beyond the norm. Major disruptions have occurred in industries such as print media, translation services, employment recruiters, hoteliers, manufacturing and the car industry with driverless cars. Thinking outside of the box has resulted in numerous developments, many of which are hard to keep up with. Sometimes, the inability to keep up with change occurs because fear of the unknown has become so great that it hinders our ability to get on board as quickly as we need to. Therefore developing an open mind and being curious is vital for organisational survival and longevity.

However, curiosity isn't limited to your external world such as the people around you, the organisation you work in or future possibilities and opportunities. It also applies to you personally. Remember that lovely (old) model called the Johari window (Luft & Ingham 1955)? It uses a simple grid to plot adjectives as 'known/ unknown to self' against 'known/unknown to others'. Ask yourself, how often do you deliberately investigate your blind (self) window – the part of you that others can see, yet you are unaware of, to deliberately explore your untapped potential? How curious are you about yourself and your future? There are many ways to develop curiosity. One way to learn more about your blind (self) window is to read diverse sources of information and develop what's known as a T-shaped mind. This is where you become a discipline specialist, with a depth of knowledge, skill and expertise (the stalk of the T) while also obtaining a broad range of more generalist skills at less depth (Guest 1991). This will help you become an expert in what you do, yet still have knowledge of other fields and disciplines. It will also help you develop a greater sense of what you're interested in and greatly enhance your creativity as wider knowledge helps you to see and make connections between knowledge areas that you would've been unable to see before. Another way to explore your blind (self) window is to seek feedback.

Most of us are scared of giving and receiving feedback but instead it should be recognised as one of the biggest gifts someone could give you or you can give to another, so long as the feedback has a positive intention behind it. The fear you feel about it is partly due to being a complex human being with hang-ups and issues, where feedback can sometimes feel like rubbing salt into an open wound, making you face things you know about yourself yet have tried to hide. When you're feeling insecure or overwhelmed, you're more likely to take on board feedback from anyone and everyone, focusing purely on the negatives. When you're feeling psychologically safe and, as we shall see, personally resilient, you have more confidence to be discerning. You'll only take on board feedback from those most qualified to offer it – namely, those people that you respect. If feedback is from a disrespected source, why would you want to take that on board?

However, when those you respect do offer you feedback, you know there's likely a positive intention behind it. Their feedback will be predisposed to help you explore that blind window so that you can develop and grow. Feedback is often the very thing everyone else can see that's holding you back, yet you can't see it for yourself. Therefore, don't be afraid of feedback. Simply develop your ability to distinguish between well-meant feedback from respected sources and feedback that may be intended to hurt or embarrass. In the latter case, remember it's highly unlikely that you'd want to model yourself on these ill-intentioned sources, so let such negative feedback roll off you. Challenge yourself to be brave and proactively seek feedback – foster greater curiosity about yourself, as this will help you develop a richer perspective about yourself.

Change your perspective

One of our research participants said that people change for two reasons: love and pain. This interesting view is something we can concur with, particularly when seen through the lens of fear – fear of losing love, fear of the pain it can cause, fear of being fired, fear of being financially insecure, fear of rejection, fear of failure, fear of change and so on. Of course, we know change happens in an instant – it's that precise point in time that you stop doing one thing and do another. However, the journey to get to that point may be perceived as long, painful and fraught with fear.

A perspective is a particular view or attitude towards something or someone, often constructed in your mind as the result of yours, or others', experiences. As Robert Dilts says, flexibility and adaptability come from having choices; wisdom comes from multiple perspectives (Dilts et al 2012). Thus, choosing to step out of your own autopilot perspective will enable you to see situations differently and, more importantly, choose how to respond to those situations to give you the best possible outcome.

However, what happens when the love or pain is simply not intense enough to motivate a change in perspective? Human beings tend to take the path of least resistance, being hard wired to default to the negative to survive. If the pain attached to the fear isn't that great you simply hold on to your autopilot perspective and respond to the world accordingly, hence the notion that you'll always get what you've always got. To get something different requires you to challenge how your brain thinks by updating that inner story and behaving differently. This requires a change of perspective.

As we saw in an earlier chapter, how the human brain processes information means much of that information coming into your brain through your five senses gets deleted, then distorted, then generalised. That means your perspective is built on a limited, individual interpretation of the world.

That doesn't mean that your interpretation or perspective is wrong. However, being able to not only develop alternative perspectives but also retain the best of your own perspective *plus* the best of another's, is one way of fast-tracking you along the pathway of developing psychological safety. You'll feel safer because other people's perspectives aren't necessarily a threat to you or your sense of value, which, as you'll see, is fundamentally important to every human being. People will feel safer around you because they know you value *their* perspective. This means you can tap into the strengths of others, be more open to creative ideas and become more innovative as a team and organisation.

An even more valuable skill is the ability to be able to hold two opposing views at the same time and to find a pathway through these opposing views to an even better solution. This ability will open the best possible route to good decisions, as you're not trying to force or choose one or other of the opposing views. Recurrently it's the dominant voice that will drive through its own perspective, possibly at the cost of some good alternative perspectives. This often ego-driven behaviour is normally based on the need for power and control, both of which can destroy any attempt to develop psychological safety. If this happens with powerful leaders at the top of an organisation, you regularly see unhelpful power struggles as egos battle it out for dominance. The lost opportunities at this level can be catastrophic, as the uncertainty, mixed messages and competitiveness trickle down through the organisation. On the flip side of the coin, the potential for creativity and innovation knows no bounds. Imagine taking the best of someone's ideas and combining them with the best of your own, with no egos getting in the way, just a healthy respect for two different yet potentially very successful ideas.

How to change your perspective

Before we even consider any of the numerous tools you might use to help you intentionally change your perspective, remind yourself that you're already able to do this extremely well. Remember when you thought Santa Claus climbed down every chimney around the world in one night delivering gifts, or that paper diaries are better than electronic ones, or that electric cars will never catch on? Views and personal perspectives change over time as a result of experience and the continuous learning it brings. What's important to remember here is that your perspective of *yourself* is coloured by how psychologically safe you feel at work. As a manager or leader, think of the impact on health, wellbeing and performance – and all the associated costs – if you multiply feeling psychologically unsafe by every member of your team. Add to this the opportunity costs – the lost innovation and creativity of people not consistently bringing their best selves to work because they've been unable to nurture their self-perception in a psychologically unsafe environment. In fact, their self-perception may have been unintentionally damaged by some aspects of your organisation's culture, procedures or ways of working, along with the lack of psychological safety needed to explore that damage. One example is line managers who are unable to develop compassion for those employees who are struggling with their mental health at work. Empathy fosters organisational affiliation and over time, those line managers unable to demonstrate appropriate levels of compassion and empathy become part of the problem as the resultant culture becomes one where the message is 'heads down, don't speak up' (Somogyi et al 2013; Meechan et al 2022). One of the most shockingly tragic examples of this is the France Telecom suicides, whereby many of the 69 employees who took their own lives left notes blaming employee relations practices (Chabrak et al 2016).

Someone else's shoes

There are numerous ways in which you can develop the ability to intentionally change your perspective. The anonymous Native American proverb 'You'll never know a man until you walk a mile in his moccasins' is a well-known one. Try to imagine you're another person, maybe someone you struggle to work with. Imagine stepping into the shoes of that person and living their life, with their challenges, issues, difficulties and pressures. Of course, we can never truly know what's going on for another person; we simply try to imagine what it must be like. However, the reward for trying will be a more rounded perspective of that person, with more empathy and understanding about why they do what they do, supporting a more compassionate response to them.

Reframing

Reframing is another useful approach to developing alternative perspectives. It means intentionally viewing a situation, person or thought from a different angle.

Figure 3: Frames of reference

Analysis of the same data, what you see in front of you, yields differing interpretations depending on your angle of view. Imagine you've been stranded on a desert island for some time. Finally, you see a boat. How would you feel? Imagine now that you'd been drifting for days in a boat and eventually you saw a desert island. How different would this feeling be to the one you just imagined as a castaway? Imagine you're a hungry shark. How different might your feeling be from the one you just imagined in the boat? This gives you an idea of how radically you can alter your perspective by first contextualising and then reframing your thoughts. Challenge yourself to zoom out and see a wider picture or change your angle of view and see the additional insights embedded from different perspectives.

Figure 4: Blind man's elephant

Learning to consciously retrieve some of the deletions by going back over the situation, asking for other people's opinions or doing more research brings back the wider context and helps to place that familiar 'small bit' into a bigger picture.

Other questions to ask yourself that will help you to reframe are:

★ What else could this behaviour, situation, thought mean?
★ What am I missing – what haven't I understood, seen, heard?
★ What might this mean if looked at with a 180° shift in view?
★ What's really going on here?

Managing your expectations

This is another important skill in changing perspective, especially among those with exceptionally high, potentially unattainable standards or perfectionist tendencies. Think of a situation, person or thought that you want to change your perspective on. Take a piece of paper and write down the answer to these three questions, being as detailed and specific as possible:

★ What is the ideal situation/person/thought?
★ What is a less than ideal but acceptable situation/person/thought?
★ What is an unacceptable situation/person/thought?

Next, rate each of your answers on a scale of 1–5, where 1 is equal to very unlikely and 5 is very likely, giving a number to the likelihood of your expectations being met. Finally, rate each of your expectations with a level for disappointment if you *do not* achieve them on a scale of 1–5, where 1 is equal to extremely disappointed and 5 is not disappointed at all.

A worked example might look like this:

* My *ideal* situation is that I can quickly execute the implementation of a new IT system and that it will work perfectly from day one. I rate this a 1 (very unlikely) in terms of likelihood of realistically achieving this. I rate this a 4 (not particularly disappointed) for disappointment.
* My *less than ideal but acceptable* situation is that I can implement a new IT system within six months and all glitches will be highlighted and resolved within the next three months. I rate this a 4 (likely) in terms of likelihood of realistically achieving this. I rate this a 2 (very disappointed) for disappointment.
* My *unacceptable* situation is that I partially implement a new IT system within a year and glitches remain unresolved six months down the line. I rate this a 2 (unlikely) in terms of likelihood of this happening. I rate this a 5 (not disappointed at all) for disappointment.

For an individual, being able to change personal perspective is key to building emotional resilience. For a team, it offers the opportunity to regard day to day knocks, failures and delays as valuable opportunities for reflection and learning. For an organisation, it offers a golden opportunity to help everyone fail faster and get to candid conversations quicker so that growth and learning can take place at a structural level.

Communicate on a human to human level

Teams and organisations

The need to 'get communication right' is watermarked into every management development course as a critical factor for organisational success. Yet year on year, results from our own assessment tools show us that communication remains a perennial source of pressure for employees, particularly from the least interactive form of communication – email. Human beings are complex with individual differences layered into a core, universal need to feel valued. The organisational attitude and approach to communication is the visible representation of the degree to which employees and their insight are *really* valued.

Knowing that people think, act and respond in different ways, it makes no sense to try and reach them all in the same manner. Communication processes need to factor in the individual communication style differences of employees. Tools available to assist, among them the Myers-Briggs Type Indicator, DiSC, Colour Works and Insights, are typically seen as interesting but navel-gazing exercises. However, these tools can be useful in raising awareness about important behavioural preferences. Ever popular, they're rarely used in one of the most important ways that they could be – to guide greater flexibility of communication style. If people don't adapt their communication style to suit the needs of those they're trying to influence and communicate with, they may be like ships passing in the night. Key messages are carried and transmitted but land incorrectly. Interpretation of the message could convey something entirely different from the intended meaning, leaving the recipient feeling devalued, angry or anxious.

Knowing there will be variability in any team regarding how psychologically safe people feel, it's worth remembering that candour and the frank, honest communication and feedback that it entails will not land uniformly well with everyone. Neither will everyone assume it's coming at thcm with positive intentions. This is especially so when people are feeling the pressure, are overwhelmed, stuck in a negative emotional dip or caught up in a drama of the moment – something we'll explore in the next chapter. Those wading in with newly found confidence to take interpersonal risks and offer up candid insights might be the very thing that pushes someone over the emotional edge.

Therefore time needs to be set aside for human to human communication on a regular basis. Organisations need to value the investment of time in understanding their people at an individual level – how they're doing individually, what pressures they're personally feeling, what concerns they personally have. No task talk! This is about them – not targets, problems, goals or achievements. As one of our research participants said, 'I want to be spoken to as a person – how's the weekend, family, etc.' It's about the creation of space and process to enable individuals to talk to their managers or team members about things that are relevant to them that may have nothing to do with their day to day tasks. It's about encouraging people to *hear* each other person, not just listening to what they're saying – valuing getting to know the human beings who happen to work in your organisation. It's about building in, as part of the working environment, time for every person in your organisation to talk about themselves. This is how an organisation demonstrates the value placed on the people who work there.

It also means working hard to be inclusive. In our consulting work we regularly undertake our own empirical research and several patterns have emerged that indicate a shift in how people perceive psychological safety within their own organisations. One such pattern is the prevalence of a view that inclusivity is strongly connected with psychological safety. However, inclusivity – an extremely important factor in helping any human being to feel valued – means different things to different groups of people. For example, some people view inclusivity at work as being valued without having to conform. One example from our own research showed that some minority groups feel they lack the right platform in their workplace to be able to communicate, speak up, have difficult conversations or feel trusted to believe their views are seriously considered. Some examples of difficult conversations cited were: exclusionary language, the pronouns people use or discussion and debate regarding non-Christian holidays.

Therefore detailed consideration of exactly *how* the organisation and teams can make every person feel included is vital. One way of doing this is to create feedback loops to discover where *exclusivity* is perceived. It's hard to address it if you don't know it's there. People's own behavioural habits and preferences often make them blind to the impact that even a single choice of one word over another can have, so this feedback is vital. Another route is to create safe spaces in which people can call out unhelpful or offensive language and behaviour. If implemented across all levels and areas of the organisation, especially if such language and behaviour stems from those at the top, such initiatives can hugely enhance the ability to communicate openly and freely about issues that may currently be under wraps.

Individuals, managers and leaders

An important point emerged in our research recently: the need to feel comfortable in your own skin. Once achieved, this powerful enabler reduces pressure to put on a work mask or pretend to be somebody you're not simply to fit in. When uncomfortable in their own skin, people feel the need to dress up what they really think or feel, resulting in them being disingenuous and inauthentic. In tandem with creating spaces for both teams and individuals to conduct human to human communication, it's equally beneficial for every individual within the organisation to take personal responsibility for working on the insecurities preventing them from speaking up authentically.

Many people, especially early on in their careers, feel insecure about themselves, about being open and taking risks. One participant in our research said that everyone needs to go on a personal journey to feel safe in their own skin, 'Because you can't show up to work as the best version of yourself if you always carry the fear of failure or the fear of being sacked with you.' This individual had a personal epiphany when she decided that she would no longer live in fear. She asked herself, 'What's the worst that could happen?' Her answer was that she could get fired – feeling secure in that knowledge she found it liberating, enabling her to speak up and be herself. She acknowledged the discomfort of the negative effects of living and working in fear and this motivated her to let go of that fear and communicate authentically.

Collaboration

Even if a few people might choose to shut themselves away in their ivory towers, people don't generally work in isolation. Cooperation and collaboration are essential features of all organisations, ensuring that the cogs of the corporate machine continue to mesh and turn. As referenced in the section on communication, getting to the root cause of workplace issues such as mistakes, failure, under-performance, toxic relationships or declining wellbeing means focusing beyond the task and the employee and concentrating instead on the human being that sits behind them both. When this happens, the ability to collaborate with others to find solutions increases.

Collaboration isn't simply a reciprocal relationship – if you do this for me, I'll do that for you. It's the ability to work and cooperate with others to produce something that, hopefully, will be better than the result you'd get from working alone. The whole becomes greater than the sum of the parts because the collaborative process creates an interplay of perspectives, experience and knowledge, whereby people from inside and perhaps outside the organisation can see and explore different elements of a problem. It helps to reach conclusions that go beyond what Shawn Callahan, founder of Anecdote, refers to as 'the limited vision of what is possible', enabling the emergence of new and better solutions (Callahan 2018). Collaboration paves the way for new communication channels, bringing people, teams and organisations close together, boosting morale and retention and leading to greater efficiencies.

As Callahan points out, there are three types of collaboration: team, community and network. Common features of team collaborations are clear goals, timelines, reciprocity and task inter-dependencies. Achievement of the goals requires all team members to complete their interdependent tasks in a timely manner and to an expected standard. Although there's often an explicit leader, team collaboration sees all members cooperating equally and receiving equal recognition. Team collaboration isn't limited to members of one internal team. There can be both internal and external partners as part of the same cross-functional collaborative team. In these instances, it's important to ensure roles are clearly defined and a clear mandate is understood by all team members.

Community collaborations are different in that they often explore shared areas of interest or domains, with less clearly defined goals. Here the focus is more often on the learning process rather than the result. In these cases, community members build knowledge with a view to solving problems rather than completing tasks. The community can often be seen as a receptacle of knowledge and experience from which questions may be asked, advice given and implemented back with the member's own team. It's clear to see the potential for shared learning, knowledge and ultimately solving some of the more challenging problems associated with improving 'broken' organisational cultures and systems by drawing on the experience of the wider organisational community.

Network collaborations often begin with individual action and self-interest. Over time they accrue a network of individuals who each contribute to, or seek something from, the network. There are rarely specific roles, power is distributed and timeframes are open and unbounded. Given the explosion in digital information, networks have become a vital part of information management and enable diverse individuals across the globe to connect. These networks have become mechanisms for filtering, capturing and creating knowledge and although each network member may be acting in self-interest, they're still providing a network-wide benefit.

Regardless of the type of collaboration you seek, to be successful there are collaborative practices that need to be embedded (Gratton & Erickson 2007). First, ensure you have executive support for the development and maintenance of social relationships. Second, create HR practices engineered to support collaboration, including reward systems, training, performance management mechanisms plus coaching and mentoring programmes. Third, ensure team leaders are major catalysts in collaborative behaviour – they need to be flexible enough to be both task and relationship oriented at varying times during a project. Fourth, structure the team or group in such a way as to expedite building trust. This takes time, especially if people don't know each other and are unclear about who does what and what needs to be achieved.

Finally, whether your collaboration is synchronous in real time or asynchronous over different time zones, the common thread throughout is that regardless of *how* you collaborate, you're building emotional connections with others. When integrity, strong values, self-awareness, motivation, participation, reflection and engagement are demonstrated, connection happens. Reciprocity in all these areas increases emotional wellbeing as people feel supported and valued by a sense of belonging to a collaborative group. This gives rise to greater self-confidence – the last behavioural fundamental to be examined but possibly the first among equals.

Confidence

Given that psychological safety enables people to speak up at work, challenge their colleagues – even their boss – and put forward their own views and opinions, it would be easy to conclude psychological safety and extroversion are contingent on each other. Amy Edmondson's research (2019) has shown that this is not the case – psychological safety isn't correlated with extroversion, or introversion for that matter. Confidence can be defined as an internal feeling of security attained when you and your capabilities are realistically validated and can be shaken if you depend on external validation from others. This is why it's so important to develop a level of congruence and authenticity about yourself. When confidence wavers, you become more susceptible to external pressures chipping away at your self-esteem, your belief in your ability and your sense of self-worth. When this happens, you're more vulnerable to being caught up in negativity at work, being drawn into the drama of the moment and sometimes fast-tracking yourself to overwhelm and burnout. Of course, confidence isn't just a personal feeling. It's also extremely important to have confidence in your colleagues and your line manager. Confidence in others reflects your own sense of self-confidence and is built through trust – trusting each other to do a good job, to have each other's backs, to speak up when there's a problem, to praise when something goes well, to not make you feel stupid. When everyone is confident in each other, trust multiplies.

Developing confidence in other people comes by consistently validating and recognising the specifics of everyone's contribution to team success, helping all team members see their colleagues as valuable and important. Each team member plays a role in assisting their colleagues to grow in confidence by actively building them up, as well as (constructively) calling out behaviour designed to knock them down. Such destructive behaviour can potentially push people towards overwhelm, drama or burnout. Building people up requires celebrating successes, creating opportunities for reflection and learning, acknowledging the need for improvement, setting tasks that help stretch people and being sensitive to those who may feel in a prejudiced minority. This is, of course, exactly what a climate of psychological safety enables teams to do. Therefore everyone needs to play an active role in its development.

One area that we've noticed in our work with many multinational organisations is that many non-native English speakers working for westernised organisations can feel at a disadvantage because of language differences. This can manifest itself in a lack of confidence and ultimately a lack of self-esteem. One of our research subjects said they felt 'there [was] a bias around English speaking' demonstrating that, as a non-native speaker, there are additional challenges to feeling heard that can undermine or bruise already fragile confidence and which are largely invisible to native speakers. Therefore being sensitive to this possibility and asking the right questions to uncover the reasons why confidence may be low is important. This way everyone can play their part in improving individual and ultimately team confidence, making it much easier to tap into the embedded creativity and innovation waiting in abeyance.

One final area to mention is the need for shared confidence in the organisational system itself – the policies, procedures and working practices that support people to do their jobs. In our work we often come across excellent policies, carefully engineered to support longer-term employee wellbeing and sustainability, eg dignity at work, career breaks and agile working policies. However, we also hear frustration from some employees who see the uneven or unjust implementation of such policies. Sentiments such as 'Agile working doesn't apply to us in field sales' or 'They sit in their ivory tower offices and don't care that we work a 16-hour shift with no shelter' or 'We only get a 20-minute lunch break on the production line' are clear indications that policies do not necessarily meet the needs of all employees.

Paradoxically these gaps can go on to create resentment and undermine trust in the very policy structures designed to support and protect them. These complex systemic issues are the last to be addressed, if ever. It's unsurprising then that they're in the box marked 'difficult'. Seeking to resolve these issues feels to many like opening a can of worms. Yet, as with any issue that looks unwieldy on the surface, broken down into its constituent parts it can become more manageable. Finding out exactly what, where and why there's a problem provides the information needed to address the issue where it's causing the most problems. Universal solutions create local problems.

The path of least resistance

So now you know the five key behavioural foundation stones for a psychologically safe workplace: curiosity, change of perspective, communication, collaboration and confidence. It will be clear by now that the five Cs don't act independently of each other; they overlap and have a symbiotic relationship. It will also be clear that lacing these behaviours together, even within a single role, is likely to be a journey with a few bumps, ruts and potential roadblocks along the way. Scaling that up to the organisational level may look like an impossible task but changing the minds of many requires that you first change the mind of one.

That 'one' may be you, or it may be someone else who has a lot of influence. As we have demonstrated, thinking differently leads to doing differently and although not necessarily difficult, behaving in a new way is invariably uncomfortable. As previously mentioned, humans are hard wired to feel more comfortable when things are familiar. This remains the case even when those familiar habits are proven to be bad for wellbeing and performance. Humans are drawn to keep doing the same things wherever they can because it feels easier and less uncomfortable than doing something else. People gravitate naturally toward the paths of *least* resistance – footways that are usually well trodden.

The road of more resistance

Even when you're pretty convinced it's the right thing to do, it does take a concerted effort to do something differently. It usually requires you to draw on inner resources and your strength of character and always requires you to move off the path of *least* resistance onto a road with *more* resistance – one that might involve pushback, potholes or roadblocks. Once off the beaten path, with fewer people (or maybe nobody) up ahead, the trail can disappear without warning and you're left wondering whether you took a wrong turn and should retrace your steps. Without a compass and a strong pair of boots, or without an underlying ability to 'back yourself', a humbling journey back to the path can await. However, with the right tools you can navigate to the top of the hill and see for miles.

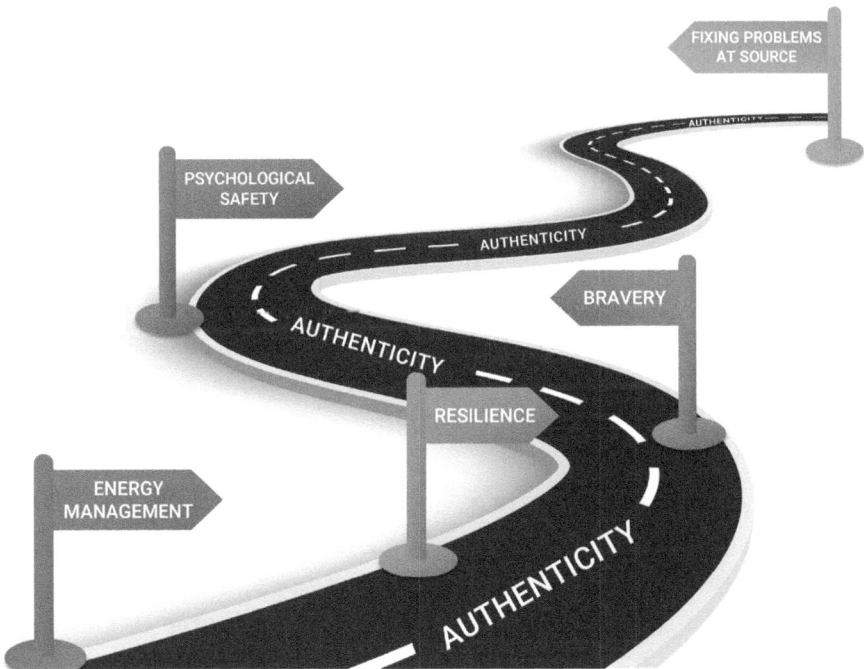

Figure 5: The road of more resistance

The (unapologetically) extended pathway metaphor has a purpose. Doing your bit to create greater psychological safety in the team by integrating the five Cs can be a chance for everyone to start doing something differently tomorrow, whether they're a leader, a manager or a team member. It's a road trip that everyone can participate in. Simple to adopt, the approaches we've just outlined may feel unfamiliar at first – a bit like folding your arms in the opposite direction to the way you normally do it. You don't need any special skills to be able to start straight away, just enthusiasm for all the benefits to be had by becoming more aware and bringing these ideas into your leadership or interpersonal interactions. However, there are conditions you can create for yourself that act as specific mile markers to keep you moving along this new highway. Some are specific enablers that will act as strong boots with good grip; others when adopted increase the ground covered and lower the journey times.

The first and second mile markers are developing an intentional approach to individual and team energy management and the role that this plays in building personal and organisational resilience. These are so fundamental to the later stages of the journey and final outcome that the whole of the next chapter is devoted to it. It's a topic worth covering in more detail because when people are allowed to be purposeful as well as physically, emotionally and mentally resilient, they're effectively able to buy themselves the time they need to put an exploitable gap between what happens to them and what they do in response. They can harness the moment of time that's always there between a stimulus and a response, to look past their own thinking habits and biases and catch themselves before they offer an unhelpful response. This is the fertile ground on which the seeds of personal and organisational change are sown and nurtured. If you can get away from the self-sustaining inertia of 'what we normally do' – in other words, cultural custom and practice – there's a 'gold dust' space. In this gap sits the opportunity for people to choose a different response and develop new strengths of character that will enable sensible challenges as new and potentially better approaches come into focus.

Emotional or mental exhaustion is the enemy of conviction. How many times have you said 'I just can't face it' about anything you felt too emotionally or physically rung out to attempt? Conversely, when you feel resilient and on the front foot, you're more likely to feel bold and confident about your insights and brave enough to voice them. This is mile marker three. In this condition you become more able to communicate and behave in the way that's necessary to contribute to a climate of psychological safety, which is mile marker four. Reaching this point makes it possible to experiment with fresh approaches and to challenge established but misfiring work habits, in other words arriving at mile marker five.

A psychologically safe working environment enables tightly packaged work problems to be properly unpacked – going beyond sliding the lid off a little and putting it back on quickly before whatever's deep down in the box has actually been taken out and examined. When leaders, managers and team members can engage in this type of open and trusting dialogue, confident that their ideas and candour will be eagerly anticipated and not just politely tolerated, everyone gets on the fast track. Enjoyable, creative and sustainable employee engagement will follow but what you also get is a clear picture of the priority areas to work on – the issues that will return the biggest wellbeing and performance ROI for the team and the organisation. A simple process for you to implement to guarantee success in this area is detailed in the last chapter of this book.

Authenticity – the soul in your shoe

Most people can recall a situation where a big 'last straw' pothole appeared in the road right in front of them and they resolved to speak out about it. In that moment they felt galvanised and ready to challenge. But a moment further on, like other similar moments, adrenaline subsided, resolve ebbed away and staying silent resumed its position as the preferred option. Honesty once again looked like a leap they wouldn't be able to make so keeping counsel and carrying on, calmly, felt like the safer option. At this point a mental bridge was probably necessary – something that would have formed itself if there was enough confidence in, and sustained focus on, what was *really* important to that person. Being true to ourselves and being able to put personal values into action, instead of constantly aspiring to live by those values next week or next month, is the true meaning of authenticity. As we saw in the first chapter, though, it's difficult for people operating constantly inside the 'must do more with less' envelope to act with authenticity. Regular conflict between what's good for the human and what's good for the employer means that sticking to what's important to you just doesn't feel like an option most of the time. Something has to give and more often than not it's personal authenticity, which is frequently sacrificed on the altar of company objectives or meeting deadlines. Very often, the steps that are taken aren't the ones that people most want to take. If they were operating from a place of authenticity, their soul might point them in a different direction.

Operating from this place of authenticity, feeling brave enough to act consistently in accordance with your values, does however require specific conditions. Doing so has its own dependencies in terms of familiarity and comfort with certain ways of behaving. These behaviours are quite specific and together they combine to build the strength of character needed to be authentically yourself. Using them fuels the strength of character needed to face down fears that might have been clouding objectivity about the sustain-ability of how you or your team are working now. Going back to the earlier pathway analogy, authenticity is effectively what you resurface the bumpy pathway with. It's the smooth surface needed to support confident progress towards the destination – a workplace culture safe enough to have real conversations about how to deliver on company-led goals *without* compromising the personal purpose and wellbeing of the people that make it all possible. These specific behaviours are the subject of the next chapter.

Chapter 5: Big questions

* If you're a **team member:** what can you do to help yourself feel more psychologically safe? How can you build your confidence to speak up authentically when you're struggling, have a great idea or want to share your point of view?
* If you're a **people manager**: how psychologically safe does your team feel? Do you even know? Can you ask the right questions, in the right way, to start your team opening up about how safe they feel?
* If you're a **senior leader**: how can you create a climate of psychological safety with your peers? How can you role model having candid conversations for middle management while maintaining trust among yourselves?

Key messages

* Creating and working in an environment of psychological safety yields both performance and wellbeing results, particularly when facing relentless pressures and demands. Enabling candid conversations where people can speak up if they're struggling and put forward ideas builds trust and collaborative bonds.
* To create psychologically safer workplaces, focus on the five Cs: **curiosity** about the causes of pressure and potential opportunities; **changing your perspective**, being open to new ideas and valuing differences by being inclusive; **communicating** human to human, talking to the person, not the task, truly seeing and hearing each individual; **collaboration**, finding opportunities to build bonds by working together to achieve results; and **confidence** in yourself, your manager, your leader, your organisation and your policies and procedures, knowing that they're helping, not hindering.
* People are vulnerable without psychological safety, often operating under a cloak of fear which at best stops people bringing their best selves to work and at worst can be toxic and destructive to both health and performance.

6 Resilience, energy and performance

You wouldn't expect a house to stay dry with half its roof tiles missing, nor would you expect to build a two-storey house with the number of bricks needed to build a bungalow. Companies rightly take a highly specific approach to the management of their supply chain but oddly, the need for reliability and continuity that drives focus in this area doesn't seem to apply to employee sustainability. While there's always vigorous agreement within senior leadership teams that employees are all individuals, at the same time they often believe that employees will be able to cope with what's asked of them, resulting in a kind of human resource homogenisation. Employees are assumed to have equal coping capacity until proven otherwise. Then there's also the troublesome assumption that they will let you know if they can't cope – but the stress statistics tell us that they don't.

As we have said, this is the approach that's often being taken and it's visible in the generalised nature of a lot of employee wellbeing and performance strategies and related provisions. There are many potentially helpful self-service interventions but a notable lack of specificity about who they will assist, under what circumstances those people will benefit and, most critically, what issue they're addressing. There's no doubt that a broader range of pressure management skills mitigates poor wellbeing, so we applaud those companies that help their employees build personal resilience. But it isn't enough on its own. It needs to be a strand in a broader strategy that also looks at what people need to build resilience for. Trying to build resilience without more detailed awareness of what people are grappling with is a little like nailing jelly to a tree. Resilient behaviours can be described and taught, and it's possible to discuss them generally and without specific context. But knowledge of what the team is struggling with or what gets in the way of them being able to bring their full selves to work is going to make time spent adopting coping behaviour feel much more relevant. It's also much more likely to drive sustainable behaviour change.

Helping your human resources build personal and team resilience makes sound business sense and, given that the behaviours involved pay equal dividends in responding to life events in general, it's also a good thing for talent development and employee capability. But without data, knowing where to start can be problematic, particularly if you have no specific understanding of what they might need to become resilient to other than the ubiquitous heavy workload. This difficulty is compounded by the fact that there's no universally agreed definition of what resilience actually means. Psychologists define resilience as our process for adapting and remaining strong in the face of significant sources of stress or trauma. The *Oxford English Dictionary* defines it as 'the capacity to recover quickly from difficulties, toughness'. In our work we like to refer to it as the ability to be physically and mentally capable of handling what life throws at you and to retain your ability to choose your response under any circumstances. However it's defined, there's no downside to offering employees as much support as you can afford to help them adapt to change, stay mentally strong in the face of adversity and retain the ability to choose the right way to react under pressure. There's plenty going on in the world of work and beyond to make this money well spent.

But even when building resilience is part of a wider wellbeing strategy, it's a mistake to think that this component is a purely personal journey and that the employee can become resilient on their own and without the cooperation or participation of the company that's paying for it. Sadly, it does sometimes look as if that's the expectation – the company puts them through a course and hopefully they'll become less stressed about what they're being asked to do. Building resilience in the workforce is a multi-level, poly-stakeholder activity. All parties have responsibilities and need to play their part.

An employee's ability to take the learning they're being offered and adopt it to change their outlook and behaviour is heavily influenced by their working environment. For the classroom theory to become daily practice the workplace culture needs to be an enabling one. As we've said, humans are a highly social species. As a result, individual decision making is affected by unconscious assessment of what others are doing and the personal risk of doing something that's different. The context in which resilience training is offered is therefore crucial to its efficacy – it's no good teaching employees about the power of strategic recovery and encouraging them to change their behaviour accordingly if manager behaviour suggests he/she/they don't believe this to be 'real' or a priority. It's therefore obvious that for resilience training to be effective, the managers and leaders of the participants need to role model those same resilient behaviours themselves. By doing so they give permission for team members to break some unhelpful habits and behave differently.

This happens much less often than it should. Leaders are often deselected from the training because it's assumed they already know 'how to do it' – their rise to a leadership position being taken as proof of the fact. In this circumstance, when team members return from training, their manager can't visualise what they've been learning or what they may be trying to integrate into their lives. This being the case, they're unable to model or support those same behaviours. As a consequence, employees notice that their newly acquired commitments to small step behaviour change are neither mirrored nor actively encouraged by their manager. They therefore quickly default back to the 'safer' old habits and responses. Things then progress much as before except that now there will be a new level of frustration and ultimately cynicism that 'I could or should be doing this differently but am prevented from doing so' or 'I know there is a better way to respond to this but what's the point?'

The connection between developing employee resilience and

improving psychological safety is easy to see. Personal development of any kind invariably means personal change which, given humans' natural wiring for repeating behaviour that has worked up until now, is hard under any circumstances. Add in the natural drive to align behaviour with what everyone else is doing and the fear of consequences that may result from a departure from that local norm and it's obvious why so many post-workshop good intentions flounder. Rarely is it solely explained by a lack of will or interest on the part of the trainee – there are other stakeholders involved and their influence is as direct as it is unconscious. More green shoots of personal change are crushed by a lack of peer or manager comprehension than by active resistance but the result is the same. It has to feel safe to do something differently and people often don't feel brave enough to risk it, even when they know it's the right and personally sustainable thing to do.

The happy news is that even a small positive shift in perceived psychological safety instantly increases the return on existing training investments. Augmenting resilience at the individual employee level starts with leaders and the people themselves having a sharper appreciation of the many conflicting demands and pressures embedded in modern life. These were discussed extensively in Chapter 2, alongside the impact that pressure to keep doing more with less has on stress and burnout. Complementary to this understanding is the knowledge that under pressure humans become even more likely to respond to demands in habitual ways. The more pressure turns to stress, the more likely they are to choose a response that's familiar. But what feels familiar and therefore normal may not be the best response from either a performance or a wellbeing perspective. Moths are drawn repeatedly to lightbulbs at night but burning their wings on hot glass has unintended but predictable consequences for their ability to keep flying. Organisational resilience is no different. Until recently, apart from the rapid acceleration of the pace of life and work precipitated by 'around the clock' connectivity, the underlying business model hasn't changed much. Within this well-established framework, local cultures and embedded narratives develop, shaping collective expectations and opinions about what is or isn't possible. This operating environment feels real and, as we saw in the first chapter, is self-sustaining. But just like individual habits, the narratives that shape organisational culture are fully available for challenge and revision by anyone capable of looking up and over these well-worn habits and assumptions. A resilient organisation ritually and intentionally looks for ways to review, challenge and update established thinking, folding in and leveraging new information as it becomes available in order to present the most alert and informed face to its corporate challenges. As Elon Musk never tires of telling the world, 'Something is only impossible until somebody does it.'

A resilient organisation has agile processes and procedures and is flexible enough to adjust to meet the varying demands of a diverse workforce. It has agile systems that can be adapted to meet the needs of local workgroups and teams. It has agile roles and ways of working, enabling individuals to craft their own jobs in such a way that plays to their strengths. Crucially, it cultivates agile mindsets, able to respond adaptively to fluctuating levels of pressure. There is, then, an infinity loop at play. In order to be agile and resilient, the company needs to organise itself and support its employees in a way that intentionally and specifically enables them to meet the challenges of work and life head on by being fully and authentically themselves. When the whole human is employed, trusted and respected – not just the skills bit – then the whole human can contribute at work.

The critical thing to know about personal and organisational resilience is that over time it increases performance capacity. We recruit and train for job competencies but all the skill and competence in the world is of no use if you're too exhausted or fearful to bring what you have to the table or feel compelled to hold back a large portion of your knowledge and insight. If people are encouraged to be self-aware about what they naturally do as well as admit the possibility that there may be alternative ways to 'use' their personal resources in the workplace, then an increase in performance capacity can naturally follow. The critical factor is the last part – they feel safe to do so because they can see their leadership behaving in the same way.

Resilient employees who have the spreading roots we spoke of in Chapter 1 can maintain engagement throughout the storms of work and life. As employees lean into work challenges and become even more engaged, they dig deeper and deploy even more of themselves in response. This is a very different response to simply throwing more (usually unpaid) hours to get through. Resilient employees have developed the skills to hold multiple perspectives and regulate their emotional response when faced with adversity, growing through it rather than merely surviving the experience. As a result they waste fewer internal emotional and mental resources, diverting them instead to sharper focus, more innovation and more confident experimentation (as their third creative brain comes out from beneath the previously dominant risk-averse chimp brain). When employees deploy their internal resources in this way there's less waste, as energy and attention are intentionally directed to places where there will be a better direct return on the energy and attention invested. This is how it becomes possible to do more with less, to a high standard and with a better quality of life. From the position that many people are starting from today, this may sound like an impossibility but it's highly achievable.

Creating a culture for resilience

For an individual to become optimally resilient, they need to operate within a resilient culture. This means a culture where each person they interact with has the same understanding of what that means in behavioural terms and they're confident that awareness exists because they can see their colleagues and manager doing the same. Inside a resilient organisation there's a shared enthusiasm for both the personal and the business benefits of behaving this way and *everyone* takes responsibility for using their unique and scarce personal resources mindfully and in intentional ways. The key word here is everyone, because creating a culture for resilience needs to involve all levels of staff and leadership. At the most basic level employers have an obvious duty of care, under regular health and safety legislation, not to damage employees in the course of their work. The first line of defence against psychological damage at work is paying attention to potential primary sources of pressure – a vital part of any wellbeing strategy. This is an activity that should be led from the top even if the detail is fed up from the bottom (which it will need to be).

However, the employees themselves also have a specific role to play in mitigating those risks on their own account. This starts with them being mindful of their own resilience and stress tolerance and speaking up, or seeking external help if they feel they're struggling. In much the same way as health and safety campaigns are often personalised over washroom mirrors by slogans such as 'You're looking at the person responsible for your health and safety', a culture for resilience involves all parties being accountable for the choices they make and the actions they take. One of the most rewarding aspects of our training work is seeing the penny drop about personal responsibility. There's often a noticeable energy change when people realise that there are, after all, small adjustments *they can make for themselves* that will enable them to use their personal resources. This can be done in a way that will allow them to have enough of themselves left over after work for the other relationships and responsibilities that matter to them. Sometimes we see a collective dawning that what they're *getting* in their life right now might be closely linked to what they're *doing* – that the way they've been managing their personal resources may have unintentionally placed them on the back foot. This is why they feel so behind the curve all the time. Even more powerful is the realisation that although they may not be able to directly influence much of what happens to them at work, they can change the way it affects them just by slowing down their response. In short, they see for the first time that they may, after all, have some options and therefore more control than they thought.

This ability to actively choose a way to respond is central to the whole concept of personal resilience. In our complex global economy, the reach of an individual's control or influence is limited, even among the most senior people. Few people can directly influence the events they must react to but more control over how they react is available than most actually exercise. This is why emotional regulation is such an important part of developing resilience. When people are effectively hijacked by their emotions, pushing them to merely survive the moment, the range of available response options narrows, with the most readily available often being unhelpfully negative. In the end, how employees respond to demands and challenges as well as how much effort they're prepared to put into changing their habitual patterns of behaviour is a matter of personal choice. It often comes down to how much they want a better outcome *and* whether they're close enough to the middle of the pressure performance curve to be able to make the adjustments. Unfortunately, once people feel overwhelmed, their ability to adapt their behaviour without help is compromised, which is the key reason why so many people make use of company support services. They already know they may not be able to bring themselves back to the point where they could get a better result on their own.

However, the more people that see the benefits of an adapted response and still have the emotional and mental bandwidth available to develop themselves in this way, the more resilient the culture will become. The more central building and supporting personal resilience becomes to a culture, the more self-sustaining it will be. What gets rewarded gets repeated, in much the same way that what's punished gets avoided. If it looks important enough to everyone else, then it's much more likely that people will feel safe enough to try different ways of working. They will be more accountable and intentional about how they use their personal resources on a daily basis and put effort into changing the things that they can change.

Front foot and confidence

We don't think it's an overstatement to say that an organisational culture for resilience is the foundation of employee wellbeing, performance sustainability and business reliability. It should therefore occupy a corresponding position in leadership thinking, organisational development and HR policy. However, as we've pointed out, it's a multi-layered ambition, requiring stakeholders at all levels to appreciate and *actively engage* in specific behaviours, every day. Some cat herding skills are going to be needed to move from idea to reality but a journey of a thousand miles starts, as it always has, with a single step. But these are steps that anyone can take. Starting today, every employee and manager has the ability to lead the charge by focusing on the one area over which they have unlimited control – themselves. They can look more closely at what they're doing and the choices they're making in the process of all that doing. There are myriad personal wellbeing benefits to becoming more resilient but one in particular is getting fit for the challenges ahead, both individually and collectively. It's great to be personally resilient but offering teams or workgroups the opportunity to enhance their energy and resilience at a group level drives greater *esprit de corps.* In our volatile, uncertain, complex and ambiguous (VUCA) world these skills can act as both a guide and an armoury. They are as applicable to teams who are in the 'stretch' zone and thriving but want to stay that way as they are to teams that feel themselves sliding into the 'strain' zone.

The final chapters of this book detail specific frameworks and tools to help people at all levels leverage the wellbeing and performance benefits of a more resilient culture. Our approaches will enhance self-knowledge and contain practical steps to help develop the strength of character needed to embolden your thinking, deal positively with pushback or any other negative outcomes you may experience as a result of *doing things differently* on your personal or team journey. We hope the guidance will make sense in and of itself, regardless of how confident you feel at the outset, but the advice will be much easier to follow if you're already feeling resilient.

As seen at the end of the previous chapter, challenging old habits and urban myths – both in the local team and among the higher echelons – means operating from a position of personal authenticity. A clear head, a positive emotional landscape and a fully focused and present intellect will support a good outcome in any uncomfortable conversation. As author and human potential thought leader Bryant McGill says, 'Your calm mind is the ultimate weapon against your challenges.' Authenticity requires a degree of robustness and having your energy resources under control will give you the stout foundation you need. Life will be easier with the fundamentals of resilient behaviour in place and that will help you to feel confident about your ability to carry the debate forward, to be an agent for change, independently of your sphere of influence. The more skill you've already developed in this area, the more effective the approaches offered at the end of this book will be. Personal resilience is the bedrock to feeling bold enough to stand up for what you believe in, being able to properly evaluate every situation and having the resolve to keep going in the face of pushback and adversity.

What makes you, you?

We offered up several definitions of resilience at the start of this chapter, among them the one we use, that of being physically and mentally capable of handling whatever life throws at you, retaining the ability to choose a response under any circumstances and recovering quickly from upsets and setbacks. Hopefully this will be useful to you. If you feel you're already pretty resilient, you might be a little curious to know whether there's any more you could do to take yourself up to the next level. What steps or further steps can be taken to keep you forever on the front foot, leaning into challenges rather than reeling from them?

We've found people find it easier to isolate meaningful steps for themselves if they can visualise their vitality as coming from four separate but interrelated dimensions. You have a *physical presence* in the world – your organic self, visible to others in the form of your body, glued to the planet by gravity. You're objectively here – a physical presence that supports and mobilises all other aspects of you such as your *emotional landscape*. This is your much less tangible 'feeling world', which is only available to others through what they can observe of you in the physical realm. Then there's your *mental landscape*, your cognition and 'way of going', which is largely driven by your internal stories. Then there's your *purposeful side*. Your purpose is what you feel excited about, what gets you out of bed in the morning, what you care about – that part of you that pushes you along and contains all the things you find most valuable and important. While these four domains are universal to each of us, the detail of each and the ways in which these distinct but interdependent dimensions combine is of course unique to each individual. Each of these four dimensions can be viewed as having its own energy and, like currency, energy is 'spent' and 'recovered' in specific but different ways. Together they make you, you.

You're obviously a little more complex than this but we've found that the simplicity of the model makes it relatable for most of the people we use it with. It offers them an easily digestible framework with which to peel themselves back a little and find specific areas that they can focus on. When people have identified where their personal energy comes from and how energy deficits can negatively impact the way they experience any situation, they can think more clearly about how to protect and renew the different dimensions. It's a short but vital hop from here to thinking more strategically about how to manage personal resources such that *any* energy 'expenditure' produces a balancing return on investment. This is the essence of using intentional energy management to build personal resilience.

People that are personally resilient prioritise specific behaviours over others, actively choosing until the behaviour becomes a new habit in order to respond to unpredictable situations in specific ways. By doing this they're able to preserve, direct, redirect or recover energy in each of the dimensions. By adopting a more intentional approach to how they allocate necessarily finite energy resources, they can focus their attention on the areas most likely to move them towards their personal or professional goals in tandem. Doing this prevents them wasting or misdirecting energy. This is how they get to do more with the same or fewer resources, without burning out.

Not a thicker skin

The key behaviour here is 'choosing'. Personal resilience is an active and dynamic response to the world. It has nothing to do with developing a thicker skin or even mental toughness. It's not about repelling or withdrawing from outside influences in order to stay safe and protected. It is, in fact, the opposite – engaging with them but choosing an appropriate response customised to each set of circumstances. It's also a nurtured and practised approach to life's challenges rather than an innate or inherited one. There's no doubt that some people do seem to have a preference for certain behaviours that suggest innate resilience. Usually these penchants have been deliberately practised and nurtured rather than inherited. Wherever you're starting from, building greater personal resilience through intentional energy management is a skill that can be learned from scratch and developed throughout your life. This is great news because it means that everyone can join in – but the even better news is that you don't have to wait for an age to see the benefits. The rewards are often immediate.

Just how much energy you start with each day and end up with when you finish work is determined by your daily decision making. Like any other kind of natural resource, sustainability relies on renewability. Personal energy is no different. You shouldn't assume it to be limitless – you need to practise specific and intentional renewal. A workplace culture that fosters resilience rather than just saying it does is organised with energy enablement in mind. That means it's set up to facilitate people making the correct energy management choices – particularly when they're under pressure – with leaders and managers observably modelling those same behaviours. So what are these behaviours?

The energy model

Figure 1: The energy model

The purposeful energy dimension

According to Loehr and Schwartz (2006), energy capacity diminishes with both under and overuse, meaning that the energy you expend needs to be balanced with the renewal of that energy. This applies to all four dimensions of energy, illustrated above as a continuum – a continuous cycle of four energy dimensions symbiotically relating to each other. We'll begin with purposeful energy because this in itself creates drive, aiding the replenishment and renewal of energy in other dimensions – as long as you're heading towards your *true north* or purpose/direction in life (George 2010). This is something Viktor Frankl, concentration camp survivor and subsequently world-famous psychiatrist, believed to be crucial for maintaining a positive outlook (Frankl 1985). Without such, it becomes extremely difficult to meet your personal purpose and goals let alone your company's mission and purpose. As previously discussed, if you continually subsume your own sense of purpose, you'll fast-track your energy depletion and create a mismatch between your personal and professional goals, creating inner turmoil and greater pressure. This can certainly have a direct impact on your ability to live an authentic life, as you'll see in the next chapter.

Personal purpose: the human spirit

The human spirit is a powerful entity, especially when, according to Schwartz and McCarthy, our daily work and activities are consistent with our values, moving us towards feeling that what we do has purpose and meaning (2007). It ignites the flame of desire to move toward what's important to you, helping you live a congruent life in which your deeply held values align with your behaviours, inner thoughts and feelings. This sense of congruency enables you to feel comfortable in your own skin – accepting yourself, knowing your limitations, knowing your strengths and feeling OK with both. This may seem like a pipedream at present. However, creating that line of sight between what you do on a daily basis and *why* you do it is the first step to acknowledging whether the choices you make will move you in a direction that's a good fit for you, or not. You'd hope that everything you do is rewarding and enriches your life, yet we know this isn't always the case. Purposeful energy can help you reconnect to your *why*, reducing inner turmoil – 'part of me wants to do this, yet part of me doesn't' – maintaining a positive mindset, regardless of your pressures, trials and tribulations. According to Nietzsche, 'He who has a *why* to live for can bear almost any *how*.'

A starting point for connecting to your purposeful energy could simply be to create a list of everything that's currently going well in your life, no matter how small or apparently insignificant it may appear. Every single thing on this list should demonstrate that you're taking steps forward on your journey towards your true north – even if you haven't realised it yet. The bigger picture questions around who you are and what you want from life also need to be addressed, as these will help you gain clarity about the kind of person you want to be, what you'd like your life to be like and what's important to you. Chapter 7 will help you explore some of these questions.

Additionally, you can make a list of people and things in your life that you appreciate. The 'law of attraction' claims that positive thinking brings about positive results (Mulford 1889). As such, to have positive people and things in your life, it stands to reason that there must be positive qualities about *you*, which can often be overlooked or even dismissed – especially if you feel you're not living a congruent life or are uncomfortable in your own skin. Getting to a place where you can articulate your personal mission in life or conceptualise your own true north will generate self-perpetuating and renewable energy. Thus not only will you be highly resilient when under pressure, but you'll also have the energy required to tackle those seemingly impossible tasks – for example, addressing the systemic causes of pressure within your organisation or tackling your own inner demons. Moving towards your personal and professional goals is highly satisfying.

The physical energy dimension

It feels motivating and energising when you have purposeful energy. Riding the crest of the purpose wave will, however, require a proportionate amount of physical energy to maintain. As a physical being, your energy is continually being expended and as we saw in earlier chapters your body is keen to tell you when it feels it needs renewal. You're probably equally good at ignoring it if doing so isn't convenient! But despite your ability to ignore your body's requests, physical energy is finite and must be renewed. If you do this with consideration, your physical energy can be maintained throughout the day and form a springboard from which to subsequently increase both emotional and mental energy. The elements of physical energy that we need to pay attention to are well documented and include four key elements:

1. **Nutrition** – eating for energy, which means maintaining stable blood sugar levels to avoid rollercoaster sugar rushes and sugar slumps and ensuring the energy in the food you consume lasts you as long as possible throughout the day. Importantly, as we shall see, nutrition is also linked to your emotions.

2. **Hydration** – continuous throughout the day to maintain healthy organ functioning, boosting your physical energy and reducing symptoms of dehydration such as increased headaches. If possible, try reducing caffeine and alcohol consumption, which can quickly drain your physical energy and impair your sleep.

3. **Sleep** – the biggest single aspect of physical energy that can improve your overall wellbeing or undermine your wellbeing should you have chronic poor sleep. Sleep affects your ability to physically function, emotionally cope with life and cognitively process information and produce quality outputs.

4. **Exercise** – the World Health Organization recommends 150 minutes of moderate exercise (for example, walking at a good pace) per week. Break this down into the three main categories of exercise (see below) and that means 50 minutes of each per week. Breaking it down further, this works out at 7.25 minutes per day per category. That sounds much more doable!

✧ Cardiorespiratory – incorporating the cardiovascular system. Exercise that gets you hot, sweaty and out of breath, maintaining and improving your respiratory and vascular systems.

✧ Strength – not just strengthening your muscles (which contain your energy cells) but also strengthening your skeletal frame to give you strong bones, avoiding osteoporosis as you age.

✧ Flexibility – the key to mobility. Mobile joints, especially the vertebrae (because people often sit in front of screens for long periods), along with flexible tendons and ligaments, plus a supple circulatory system, which calcifies and becomes brittle with age.

It's also well documented that exercise is linked to cognitive functioning such as the increase in cerebral blood flow, thus supplying a greater level of nutrients – glucose, oxygen, etc – to the brain (Petruzzello et al 1997).

Getting these four basic aspects of physical energy right will not only increase your capacity to get things done; it will also energise you to stay on track towards your personal and professional purpose and goals, despite life's curveballs. Additionally, you'll find yourself on the front foot for handling what life throws at you at the emotional level.

The emotional energy dimension

For two key reasons, in terms of resilience, emotional energy is a biggie. The first is that the inability to regulate your emotions directly affects your ability to access the mental capacities you were hired for. Second, like many other scarce resources, emotional energy should be used well and directed where it can produce a return on the investment. Losing control and falling into the grip of negative emotions (and potentially getting stuck in the emotional dip, or pushed to overwhelm, as discussed in Chapter 3) is hugely expensive in energy terms – for you individually and also for your team. Negative emotions radiate out rapidly like ripples on a pond. Accomplishing more with the same or fewer resources involves avoiding waste – and being stressed, frustrated or angry is as exhausting as it is unproductive and wasteful.

Accepting this, along with the knowledge that everyone is ultimately responsible for their response to demands (even though it often feels as if other people are making choices for you) is the first step towards getting more intentional about the control and use of emotion at work. Helping team members and their managers to become more emotionally literate – more aware of their emotional range (positive to negative) and what their triggers are – is an important part of harnessing emotional energy to work for the team rather than against it. When this happens, everyone becomes accountable for how they react and respond to the behaviour of others, to the situations they find themselves in and to their resilience to everyday pressures.

When lacking emotional energy, you become more vulnerable and sensitive to negativity – both your own and others. When positive emotional energy is waning, recognising that every human being has a fundamental need to feel valued becomes critical. This is because you're much more likely to take every little thing personally if you're feeling undervalued, and that can come from multiple and sometimes unlikely sources. On the face of it, it may not seem as if simple things such as shifting deadlines, lack of clarity or your work being criticised or ignored are things that devalue you. However, emotions sit at an unconscious level – for example, you don't say to yourself, 'Now I'd like to be angry.' Your emotions are unconsciously triggered by the words, actions and omissions of others, the situations you find yourself in and, of course, your thoughts.

The word *triggered* has recently become very popular. This is a positive recognition of how people are becoming more emotionally aware. However, the development of emotional intelligence also requires the ability not only to recognise when you've been triggered but also to do something about it if the response is unhelpful. It's this second, crucial stage of emotional development that's often lacking. Wearing the trigger label like a badge of honour can lead others to perceive an individual as arrogant, especially if their response is damaging to others. Saying 'Everyone knows what I'm like when I get triggered' is not a demonstration of emotional intelligence; it's a demonstration of petulance and even a move towards feeling victimised.

The drama triangle
Karpman's drama triangle is a useful model to explain how a lack of positive emotional energy can push you towards behaving in negative ways (Karpman 2019). When triggered, your behaviour can often fall into either victim or persecutor roles. It can even push behaviour toward the rescuer role.

* The victim feels powerless and helpless, having a 'poor me' stance, discounting their own sense of worth and value. They moan and complain, manipulate and avoid taking accountability for their own actions, instead seeing others as responsible for how they feel, which is often trapped, dejected and inferior to others. Being stuck in a victim mentality disables their ability to problem solve and see themselves as competent and able to change their situation.
* Alternatively, the persecutor blames others for not doing things correctly, criticising, judging, punishing and discounting the value of others. They often behave in a superior, rigid or belittling way. They feel as if they must win at all costs and avoid being made to look stupid by trying to control everything and everyone. They can also become defensive if blamed, switching into victim mode.
* The rescuer, interestingly, leans towards demonstrating helpfulness and caring to both the victim and the persecutor. However, what's actually happening is a need to be needed, driving behaviour that keeps drama ever present. This is wasteful and can be highly destructive. The rescuer validates the behaviour of both victim and

persecutor by offering attention and sympathy to the victim and agreeing with and supporting the behaviour of the persecutor. They can even become a persecutor, becoming angry if their rescuing efforts fail to achieve, which they will!

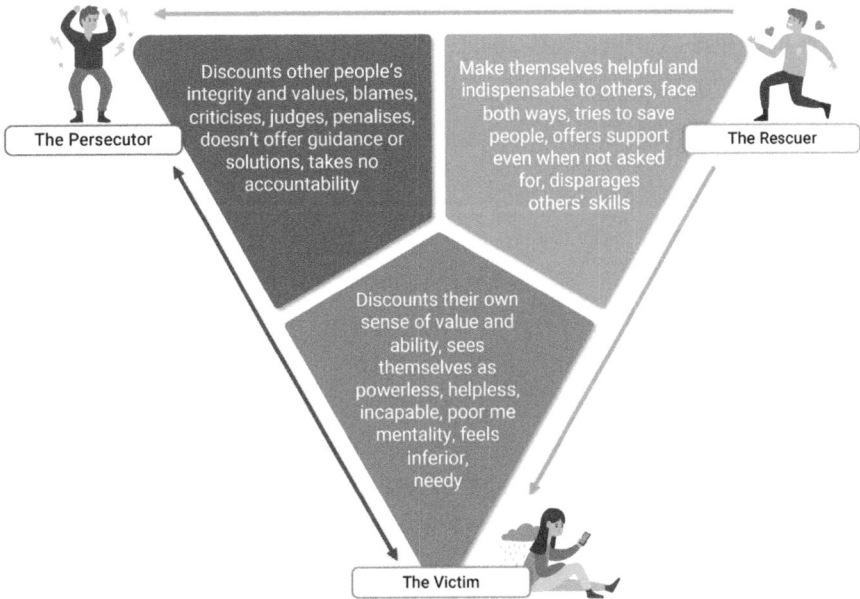

Figure 2: Karpman drama triangle

When caught up in any of these three roles, often due to a lack of feeling valued, drama continues on a loop, escalating the behaviours, drawing others into the drama and making you feel even more unconsciously devalued. Once raised into your conscious awareness, it's easier to step out of the drama triangle by developing emotional intelligence.

Developing emotional intelligence

If you have positive emotional energy, it offers choices about how to respond to life's dramas and grows from developing emotional intelligence. Here you recognise that other people can't give you an emotion. Their behaviour can trigger your emotional response

– depending, as we saw in Chapter 3 with the face model of communication, on how you perceive it and think about it. You can then express your thoughts through your feelings and finally through your behaviour. It's worth defining emotions, as in order to regulate them you need to be clear about what they are, where they come from and why we need them.

* ★ **WHAT** – emotions start as sensations within the body, which is why nobody can give you an emotion. They consist of chemical hormones and peptides from glands within your own body that carry electrical charges and send out signals and vibrations, travelling throughout the body and changing the chemistry of every cell in your body (Freedman 2007). Norepinephrine (see below), serotonin (the mood regulator) and dopamine (the feel-good hormone) combine together at varying levels to create the eight basic human emotions such as fear, anger, happiness, disgust and so on.

* ★ **WHERE** – around 90 per cent of your serotonin is found in your gastrointestinal tract and 10 per cent is produced by your brain (Cleveland Clinic 2022). It's not made by your body as it's an amino acid, obtained from the food you eat. Dopamine is produced in your brain and like serotonin is also a monoamine transmitter with multiple functions including modulation of psychomotor function, cardio-vascular, respiratory and gastrointestinal control, sleep mechanisms, hormone secretion, body temperature and pain (ScienceDirect 2023). Also known as noradrenaline, norepinephrine, like serotonin, is obtained from your diet and stored in storage granules in the nerve terminals, protected from metabolising and released when stimulated. It plays a role in vigilance, fear, alertness, the fight or flight response and can impact sleep. Stress can trigger its release from your adrenal glands.

* ★ **WHY** – on one level, emotions have served an evolutionary function, helping our hunter-gatherer

ancestors survive while facing danger and needing a speedy response. On another level, still very much linked to survival, is that emotions aid our ability to communicate and connect with others (Simons 2009). In turn, this creates a sense of belonging and hopefully a feeling of being valued, which is a core emotional need.

The emotional energy quadrant model

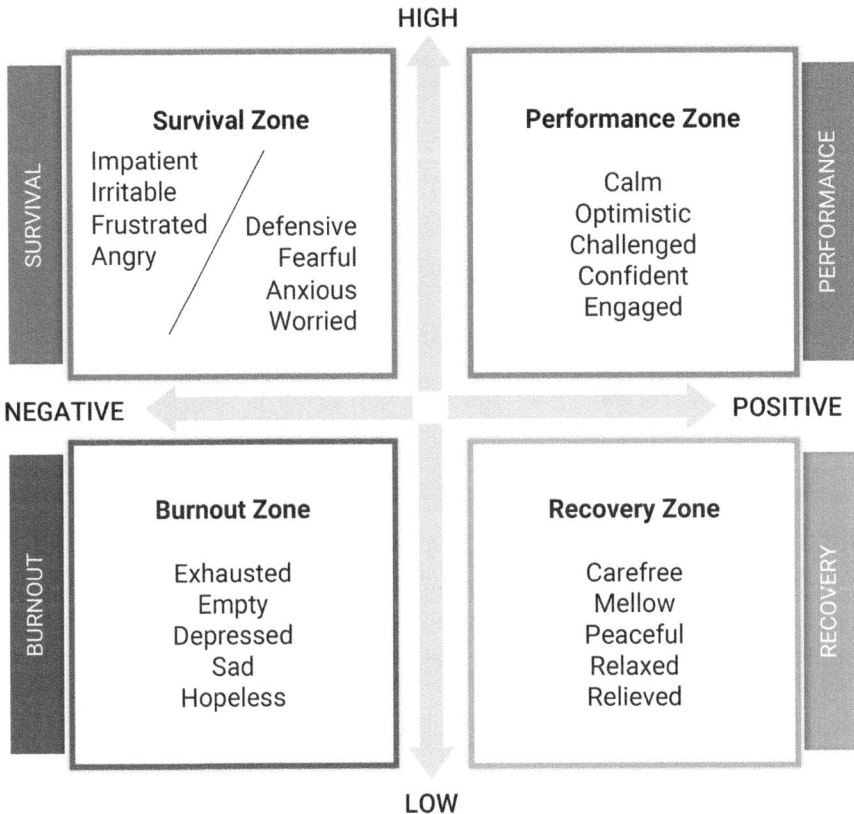

HIGH

	Survival Zone	Performance Zone	
SURVIVAL	Impatient Irritable Frustrated / Defensive Angry / Fearful / Anxious / Worried	Calm Optimistic Challenged Confident Engaged	PERFORMANCE

NEGATIVE ← → POSITIVE

	Burnout Zone	Recovery Zone	
BURNOUT	Exhausted Empty Depressed Sad Hopeless	Carefree Mellow Peaceful Relaxed Relieved	RECOVERY

LOW

Figure 3: Emotional energy quadrant (inspired by Schwartz et al 2010)

One effective way to develop your emotional energy is to use the model above to help you gauge where your emotional energy is at any given point in time in order to make any necessary changes. It can therefore work like a snapshot self-audit tool. Think of your emotional energy as being high (lots of it) or low (not a lot of it) and everything in between – deciding where you are in that moment on that axis. Next, become aware of whether you're feeling negative or positive, again deciding at what point you'd be along that axis. By joining the two plots on each axis, you'll land in one of the quadrants. Most people can move around the model without too many problems and find that they often visit more than one quadrant in any given day. That's normal – it's getting stuck in any quadrant for a significant amount of time that can cause issues.

The **survival zone** uses a high amount of energy and is a negative place to be. In survival you do just that – survive the moment you're in, becoming myopic, focusing on immediate targets or goals, losing the ability to emotionally regulate. Associated behaviours will drive others from you, increasing your sense of isolation and disconnection. Although still able to perform and achieve results, the fallout – *how* you get results – can be damaging to others. As it uses a high amount of energy, it's unsustainable in the long term.

Once you've used your energy for survival, you're likely to slide into the **burnout zone**, still feeling negative yet without the energy to feel bothered. This apathy can lead to feeling demotivated, even depressed, and is a warning that burnout is on the horizon. When burnt out, you'll usually be off sick longer than on other occasions, sometimes equating to months, or even longer (Thorsen et al 2019). When burnt out, everyday functioning such as getting washed, dressed and fed can seem challenging. This is because our adaptive systems are overstimulated and unable to turn on and off (McEwen 1998). Personal relationships can suffer and you'll be stuck in a negative emotional 'dip'. It will often be difficult to recognise or acknowledge that you're stuck here due to energy levels being too low to objectively self-assess your current state. This means it can take quite some time to get out of this quadrant.

The **performance zone** is ideally where you want to spend around 80 per cent of your working time. This is when you're at your best, able to remain calm under pressure, maintain a positive outlook even when things don't go according to plan and remain optimistic in the face of change. Your confidence enables you to be open and honest with yourself and others and life's challenges are faced head on. However, after around 90–120 minutes, your energy will naturally start to wane. This is due to the physical needs of one of your ultradian rhythms (the oscillating patterns managing cycles of energy production, output and recovery), forming part of the 24-hour body clock circadian cycle (see Chapter 2 and Gerasimo 2020). Therefore trying to maintain an optimum level of performance without paying attention to your physical needs will result in lower performance and poorer quality outputs.

The **recovery zone**, where you should spend the other 20 per cent of your working time, becomes extremely important in your ability to maintain an optimum level of performance consistently throughout the day, while also maintaining enough energy for your non-work activities. Peak performance is reached after around 90 minutes, while by-products of your physical and mental energy such as metabolic waste, cellular debris and snippets of data build up. Ignoring your body's need for recovery results in an energetic low point – the ultradian trough. You start feeling groggy, fidgety and hungry; you zone out, unable to concentrate, and your body feels heavy. Cravings for sugary/fatty snacks and caffeine may also increase. White knuckling through these dips inevitably reduces the quality of your performance. Yet, simplistic as it seems, short recovery breaks are the answer. Free of charge, these simple breaks away from your tasks replenish your energy. Choosing a recovery task that's enjoyable, not demanding, and which enables you to completely disengage from your work task will give you the biggest payback for the time invested. Recovery breaks such as this give you the ability to maintain an optimum level of performance all through the workday as well as when you finish work. It sounds like a no-brainer and it is! Why wouldn't you want to maintain an optimum level of performance? Yet the 'I'm too busy to take a break' mentality and the feeling of guilt for choosing to recover energy and keep performance high still exists.

Using the quadrant model

Like any model, you need to be able to use it practically. Apply the emotional energy quadrant model as a self-audit tool, regularly checking in with yourself throughout the day to understand which quadrant you're in. Simply recognising that you're on the negative side of the model enables you to make a conscious decision to move back to the positive side by way of navigating yourself to your recovery zone. Intentionally undertaking an activity that allows you to let go of negativity, by disconnecting from what you're doing and instead doing something more enjoyable, will assist you in getting back to your performance zone. However, not all recovery activities were created equal. In the recovery quadrants model (Figure 4), you'll see that some activities can be highly valuable while others not so. Recovering your energy by, for example, grabbing a chocolate bar from the nearest vending machine won't be as effective as going for a walk outdoors. In fact, some recovery activities such as overeating or binge-watching TV can make the situation worse. Finding high value recovery activities that work for you is essential. Short recovery breaks can be taken throughout the day, such as:

* ★ taking a short walk
* ★ attending a lunchtime yoga class
* ★ listening to your favourite music
* ★ talking with a colleague about a funny movie.

You also need to pay attention to your longer term energy recovery – ensuring, for example, that you sleep effectively, take all your annual leave and be disciplined about staying offline. These longer recovery breaks offer a vital opportunity to disengage and renew your energy and are just as important as short recovery breaks if you're to stay sustainably energised.

When you're no longer at the mercy of your emotions, having developed the ability to recognise your emotional state and regulate your response accordingly, you'll find yourself in a stronger position emotionally. You'll be better able to regulate any negative emotions that do arise which, if unchecked, might prevent you from being able to simultaneously achieve your personal and company goals and purpose. From this position it's much easier to give yourself permission to remain a consistently high performer, to care again and get excited about the possibilities that await you in meeting your purpose.

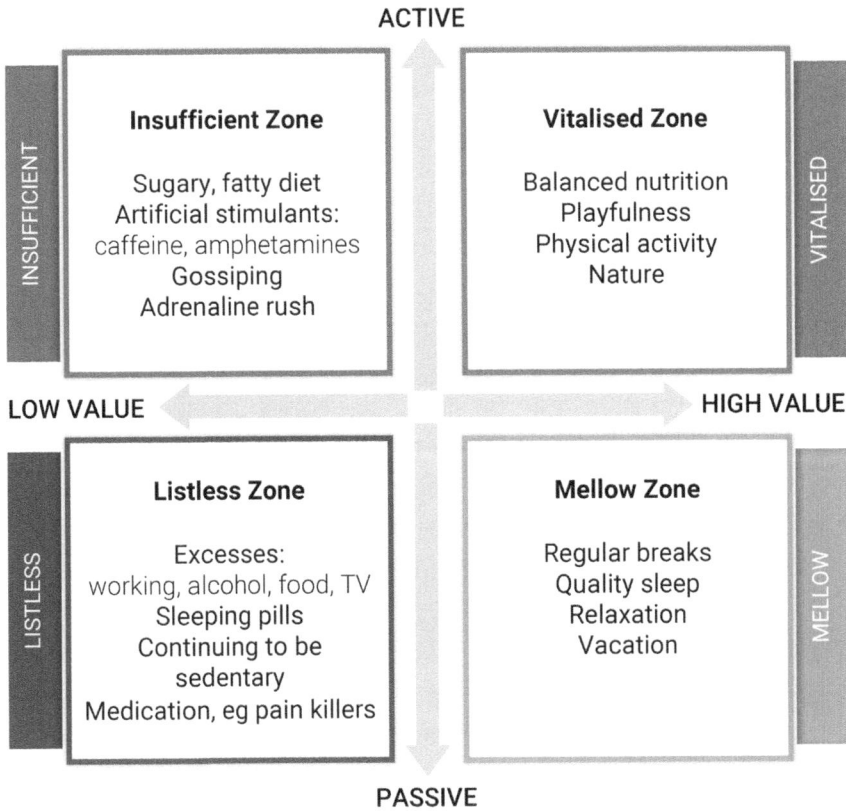

Figure 4: Recovery quadrants (inspired by Schwartz et al 2010)

The mental energy dimension

Mental energy is the key to efficiency and a cornerstone of productivity. It's how you achieve your daily tasks. To develop the capability to do your job (attaining the ability and skill to become more productive), you must combine competency (a combination of knowledge, skills, ability, behaviour and attitude) with capacity (the ability to understand information, make decisions, communicate and get things done) (Franscisco 2017). However, energy remains the missing link. A lack of energy will fast-track you to burnout as you strive to be as highly competent and capable as possible yet never achieve the level of capacity to do so. Loehr and Schwartz (2006)

149

believe that energy equals capacity – expanding your energy is what enables you to get more done in less time, with a greater level of engagement and ultimately achieving a better quality of life. You can be highly skilled and competent in what you do but without energy you'll lack the capacity to do what's necessary, continually wasting your energy with every distraction that grabs your attention.

As detailed in Chapter 2, modern life clamours for your attention and distractions are everywhere, increasing the time and energy required to complete tasks. As Linda Stone states, the information overload you face daily is based on your need to connect and be constantly connected (Stone nd). You continuously pay partial attention to what you're doing in an attempt not to miss anything. Over time, operating in this way compromises your ability to make decisions, reflect and think creatively. Eventually, says Stone, it can lead you to feel overwhelmed, overstimulated and unfulfilled because always being on and accessible actually makes you inaccessible and ultimately feeling powerless. Continuous partial attention also ensures the demise of discretionary time, which is the adult equivalent, according to Peter Pruyn, of your free period during the day (2018). As discretionary time erodes, socialising becomes a planned event rather than a spontaneous act, the quality of your attention and awareness becomes limited and you're at increased risk of becoming a prisoner of your own making. Continuous partial attention also reduces awareness, making it almost impossible to recognise when you or your colleagues are struggling, have fallen into the emotional dip or are feeling overwhelmed. This inability to be fully present limits the degree to which you can stay on track and produce quality output and, of course, limits your ability to move towards achieving those personal or professional goals that propel you on the journey towards your purpose.

Couple this with a restriction to the flip side of mental energy – innovation and creativity – and you may find yourself unable to get your creative juices flowing. The importance of creativity and its role in productivity is often misunderstood or overlooked. As such, you may be missing opportunities to reduce failure, speed it up and learn lessons, solve bigger issues or prevent yourself getting stuck in a rut. You may also reduce adaptability and therefore slow down growth. To be creative and innovate you need to be able to intentionally change your focus or, when necessary, allow your focus to become more diffuse. You can use your mental energy in an adaptive way, moving between the strategic and aerial view quadrants in the focus quadrants model (Figure 5). Here you can create space to tap into your intuition and explore limitless possibilities. It's the equivalent of having your best ideas in the shower, not being caught up in the multitude of daily distractions, or just letting your mind wander by staring out of the window – mind-fasting, as Zhuangzi put it (Fox 1996).

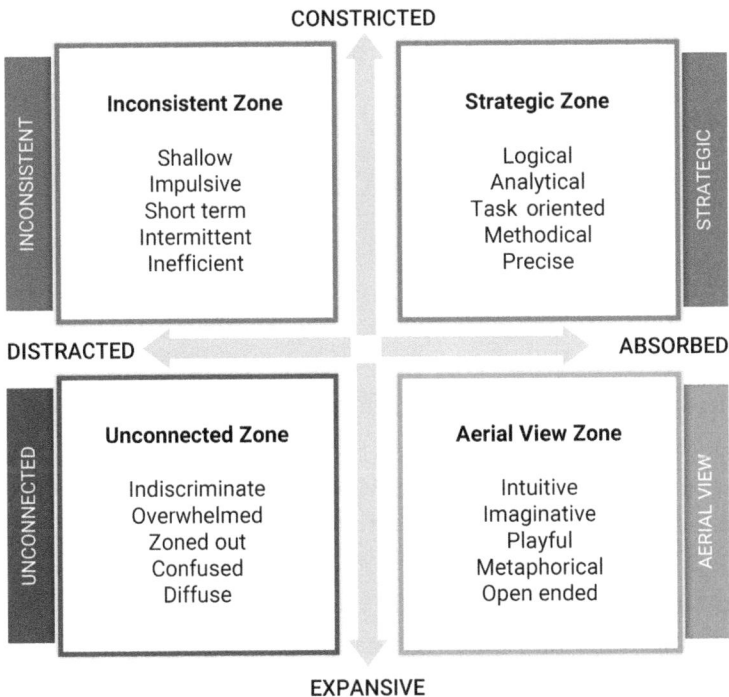

Figure 5: The focus quadrants (inspired by Schwartz et al 2010)

Increasing mental energy through the removal of distractions and being fully present clearly creates the potential not only to become more efficient, creative and innovative but to help you resolve practical conflict between personal and company goals. With every goal achieved, task accomplished and idea generated, you feel increasingly motivated, fulfilled and energised. If you think back to the pressure performance curve, you move into that optimal performance stretch zone, stepping out of your comfort zone and into a more dynamic and stimulating phase of working. This can be sustained by dipping your toe back into your comfort or recovery zone once in a while to keep your brain sharp and efficient, like sharpening an axe. This oscillation of highly focused effort and diffused open-endedness, combined with recovery, enables you to sustainably remain in your stretch or performance zone. This oscillation generates a self-fulfilling drive, permitting you to explore and expand your personal and professional purpose, circling you back to where you started with purposeful energy, yet now highly resilient and even more committed.

The magic of healthy high performance behaviours

Everyone we've ever worked with, be they conference delegates or senior leaders, is doing some of what has just been described. A very small number report that they routinely do all of it! The wonderful thing about energy management and the vital part it plays in building personal and organisational resilience is that it doesn't matter where you start. There's no external benchmark against which to measure an individual. Instead it's about each person on the team identifying the behaviours that *they* need to work on, changing habits that self-sabotage and strengthening behaviours that make use of the gap that exists between stimulus and response so that they can actively select the right response in every situation. Breaking down personal energy into four dimensions enables a more granular approach to personal action planning. However much good stuff is already going on, everyone can find something in one or more dimensions that they could be doing more diligently or more intentionally. Managing personal energy to build resilience in four distinct aspects – purposefully, physically, emotionally and mentally – gives every employee the ability to use themselves in the best way possible and grow and flourish when the pressure is on.

Getting a handle on your personal energy and developing the right habits to sustain high performance is the foundation on which everything more nuanced is built. This group of behaviours acts as your personal operating system which, once loaded and thrumming, can run and manipulate all your unique, sophisticated but often mutually incompatible 'applications'. Without it being fully up to spec, like apps on your devices, you just won't run as well and as smoothly as you could. Remember, getting personal and team energy under control is the first step towards tackling the sources of stress in your organisation. By this means you can arrive at the second mile marker – resilience.

Putting on your own oxygen mask first

Just a reminder before we move on that if you're a leader or manager you have additional responsibilities in this area. You may not have formally signed up for it but as the manager you're required to be an exemplar. Your team will be watching what you do and you're therefore obliged to demonstrate your belief in the importance of investment in resilience by role modelling the healthy performance behaviours yourself, every day. Doing so obviously contributes to your personal sustainability but even more importantly gives your employees permission to prioritise their own wellbeing and sustainability in the same way. Personal resilience facilitates self-mastery, which is such an essential part of strong and effective leadership. Managers and leaders therefore need to be doing this even better. With self-mastery a manager can choose how to respond to people and situations that might otherwise 'push their buttons' and generate a hard-wired, negative response. Just being of management grade does not provide its own automatic insulation. To set an exemplary benchmark, what's needed is self-mastery over how you use your internal personal energy resources.

Chapter 6: Big questions

- ★ If you're a **team member**: what are you doing to take personal accountability for maintaining and improving your own energy levels and building personal resilience?
- ★ If you're a **people leader**: how are you creating a culture of resilience within your team, helping them to collectively respond to pressure more effectively and be supportive of one another?
- ★ If you're a **senior leader**: which resilient behaviours are you role modelling, enabling others to 'gain permission' to do likewise by observing your own actions – ie 'If the boss does it, it must be a good thing'?

Key messages

- ★ Creating a culture for resilience is a multi-stakeholder endeavour, not a top-down initiative. It will help everyone to manage pressure at work more effectively, increasing sustainable high performance.
- ★ Resilience can be maintained and even increased by enhancing energy in all four dimensions: purposeful, physical, emotional and mental. Without resilience people become more vulnerable to getting caught up in drama, wasting energy and becoming less productive.
- ★ Energy requires renewal and as such it can become self-sustaining as long as you recover energy in all four dimensions. Not all recovery is equal, therefore effective action needs to result in high value recovery.

7 Your BRAVE new world

We must be the change we want to see in the world.
– inspired by Mohandas Gandhi

It will be clear to anyone with even a slight knowledge of the virtuous Indian lawyer Gandhi that he was authentically himself. Despite any fear he may have felt, he was bold enough to espouse his values and demonstrably live by them. In so doing he helped to ease poverty, expand women's rights, end untouchability, challenge British-imposed taxes and ultimately help India to achieve self-rule. Ask yourself, how often have you seen the epigraph above (based on his ideas) and acknowledged the truth of it, without pushing yourself to actually embrace it in your own life? Is it enough to admire and support those who visibly stand up for what they believe is right, or does it only count if you are one to be personally leading the charge?

Feeling comfortable in your own skin and being personally authentic requires courage and bravery. Acting in a way that outwardly demonstrates internalised morals, ethics and values requires a level of inner strength that many people struggle with or may need to keep working on. Feeling able to ask searching questions and challenge a system that's actively trading on the goodwill of staff and driving poor wellbeing requires a climate of psychological safety. Just feeling able to speak up with confidence about what's bothering you, or feeling fearless to try something new because you're confident your leaders and peers would view a failure as a learning opportunity rather than an opportunity to apportion blame requires the same amount of inner strength. Even if workplace conditions are 'right' for authenticity, the person with something important to share still needs to feel brave enough to actually share it. Strength of character is needed.

Human beings are complex creatures with unique and interconnected hang-ups, worries, judgements, strong emotions and related reactionary behaviours. Because of this, when people feel devalued they often react defensively, withdraw or take things personally rather than looking objectively at the situation. Building self-awareness and using it to develop personal strength of character gives *everyone* in the organisation, regardless of their position in the hierarchy, the opportunity to keep sufficiently clear-headed to speak up and contribute directly to the organisation's development. The more people there are who feel empowered and emboldened to share their unique insights, the faster the prison door of fear gets unlocked for others – a portal that, when bolted shut, consigns everyone else to operating within creative constraints. Under these circumstances, the team may unconsciously feel that there will be a risk involved in stepping outside the door. Better then to stay well inside rather than risk the career-limiting consequences. Not raising your head above the parapet, complying unreservedly (if privately grumpily) with unpopular decisions and working diligently within these unspoken guardrails in order to be seen as a solid team player is an obvious and popular strategy. Unsurprisingly, leaders with controlling or didactic tendencies are extremely comfortable with their employees taking this approach. However, a lack of articulated pushback shouldn't be taken as evidence that there is none. People's knowledge that something is wrong or feelings that the objective could be achieved in a less damaging way are very much there; they're just toxically suppressed.

In work environments that are generally psychologically unsafe, any brave bursts of openness that do occur are often received with pushback, headshaking 'disappointment' or even stealthy exclusion from future explorations of the topic. Little wonder then that the 'keep your head down and say nothing' strategy is the one most often pursued by employees, a strategy also often adopted outside the workplace. A little self-compassion should be applied here. Doing something different *is* difficult and humans aren't fond of doing it. Humans have evolved to feel more comfortable with the familiar, even when doing what's well established doesn't produce the best outcome on another axis, eg our health. People tend to make use of available resources in such a way that they can follow a path of least resistance. This makes use of the resources available yet may not be the most effective way. It takes a concerted effort to change behaviour, even when doing so would produce benefits and it's the right thing to do. Doing this on your own, departing from what everyone else is doing, is even more difficult. It's therefore easy to see how staff might readily give up on healthy high performance behaviours such as going home on time, taking strategic recovery breaks or using fitness facilities in the middle of the morning if this results in sideways looks, snide comments or unconcealed glances at a watch.

For the same reasons, the difficulty in 'being the change' can also extend to feeling confident about openly admitting missteps and mistakes. With most workplace cultures still unintentionally positioning failure as negative or a manifestation of weakness or lack of competency rather than a valuable learning opportunity, mistakes aren't easy to talk about. It's fair to assume that owning up to one may be accompanied by a penalty of some sort. Not surprisingly, therefore, sophisticated blame cultures can develop under these conditions, leading to furtive behaviour, cover-ups, abdication of responsibility, lack of accountability and denial. Unless the unfortunate employee has sufficient resilience and emotional intelligence to handle the comeback, the most likely response to discovering an error has been made will be to keep quiet about it. At best this leads to defensiveness; at worst it can be relationship wrecking or career destroying.

Robust, resilient and authentic

Because people don't generally live and work in a psychologically safe world, being open, honest and candid at work can be a challenge. Developing a psychologically safe environment where people can speak up, admit their mistakes, put forward novel ideas or positively challenge each other requires energy and resilience from multiple stakeholders, simultaneously. How comfortable people feel about being open is obviously going to vary a good deal, influenced by differences in personality, working environment and circumstances. This same variability will guarantee that the consequences of speaking up will not always be positive. A prophet is rarely welcome in their own country, after all.

This is why being robust, resilient and authentic is so important. You need to be able to absorb the knocks you encounter in response to brave openness. It will require you to tap into inner resources and build strength of character so that you can act in accordance with deeply held core values and demonstrate integrity. Then, and only then, will you be able to lean into any negativity that comes from taking small steps outside the guardrails, challenging accepted narratives in the spirit of team and organisational improvement. Pushback will not undermine who you are as a person or how you see yourself. You have the right footwear for the road of *more* resistance. Let's be honest: negative consequences do hurt but this is where the ability to manage your emotions in a way that supports objectivity becomes so important. There's no progress without failed attempts. With self-awareness comes the ability to stay in control of your emotional life when the road gets rutted. Then you're able to develop that all-important ability to stay objective and focused on the goal while keeping your emotional response to pushback appropriate. With your ability to regulate your emotions it's possible to stay mindful that personally directed negativity often says more about the person directing it than it does about the person on the receiving end. By constantly developing strength of character you're able to recover from setbacks and remain secure regarding your insights and judgements. You develop sufficient self-belief, self-confidence and self-esteem not to take any negative consequences personally.

Emotionally intelligent and brave people don't need to blame others or seek retribution for pushback either. When negative feedback is given, there are two clear response pathways, one heading towards revenge and vengeance and acting spitefully from a place of hurt and the other leading to curiosity and the ability to wonder why certain things were said or happened. Strength of character enables you to step back from personal discomfort and learn from the experience, knowing that far from being diminished by the experience you have developed and grown.

Avoiding inertia and breaking out of *expected* behaviour involves stepping into a space that's unknown and may seem scary. If there has been personal experience of hurt, rejection, humiliation or even shame as a consequence of previous candour, people are unlikely to relish the salt-rubbing potential of another go. However, if the itch to be brave and do the right thing still exists then action is necessary. Suppression only leads to anger and frustration, which in turn can lead to disengagement and cynicism towards leadership and the organisation itself. Negative emotions serve no purpose when they're held on to and are a significant contributor to stress and burnout.

Being the change

What does 'being the change' involve on a practical level? The sweeping answer is that it requires intentional steps outside the familiar, your personal comfort zone. Being the change requires the daily deployment of a series of linked behaviours that are practised and honed, peer to peer and leader to team. Like any other form of transformation, the behaviours form a practice and you need to practise them regularly to make them effective. They're not difficult to adopt as individual behaviours – each has its own obvious merit and benefits – but the magic happens when you combine them as a cohesive response to individual work and life challenges.

We have created the BRAVE model (Figure 1) to help anchor and explain the detail of the individual behaviours as well as talk about how they interrelate and support each other. Adopting the behaviours in this model will help you develop the self-knowledge and skill to build a strong inner core, deepen strength of character and give you the confidence to respond well to any outcomes – particularly negative ones. Change is uncomfortable and challenging the norms or taking a different road will feel like a bit of a tussle with fear from time to time. This behavioural model will help you keep these feelings in perspective and even use them as a source of energy to keep moving forward. Rewards for these small behavioural adaptations will be disproportionately large. As a leader or manager, doing the right thing, even if it means going against the established grain, will earn you huge respect from your team members and many of your peers. It will also make you feel good about yourself.

Having the strength of character to stay strong in the face of discord and remain committed to what you believe in even when there's dissent is what separates exceptional leaders from ordinary ones.

Ultimately this model is about getting the best from yourself and other people. Where you are in the organisational hierarchy isn't a factor in this endeavour. If you're not currently in a management role, these behaviours will help you collaborate with other team members or workgroups more effectively. Most importantly, wherever you are in your company and whatever your current role, you'll be taking the first, much needed steps to 'being the change', even if others are slower and less brave than you. As mentioned, achieving something different involves doing something different.

You may already feel you're doing much of what follows, which is great. You have an excellent foundation to work from. For you, this is a call to arms to set the bar a little higher. Take a forensic look at your established response to familiar situations and get curious with yourself. Consider whether what you normally do is making the best use of your resources or stopping you from being the best version of yourself. You might also then ponder whether by not 'being the change' you're in effect colluding with the status quo while also being diminished or compromised by it.

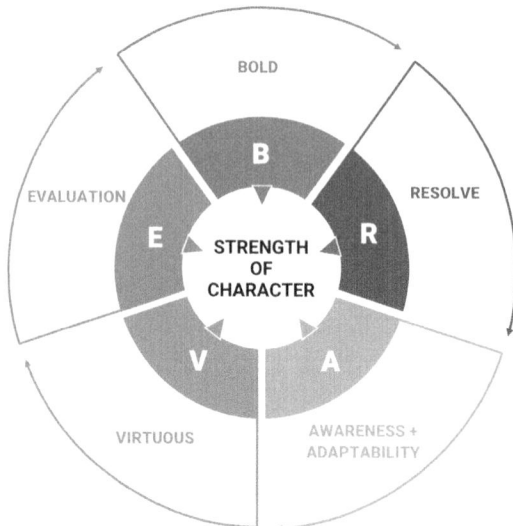

Figure 1: The BRAVE model

Step 1: Be BOLD!

To develop the courage and bravery needed to step out of your comfort zone, you must first be honest with yourself. Ask yourself, what is it that truly holds you back? What are you afraid will happen if you take that first step into the unknown? Think about your answer – if the worst were to happen, what would you do? Very often, it's the fear of the unknown or the imagined worst-case scenario that stops you being who you want to be or doing what you know is the right thing. Over time, the negative responses to your ideas, actions or beliefs can create so much fear that it paralyses you from further action. You start to lose confidence in yourself and your ability, with your self-esteem rapidly diminishing, leaving you a shell of your former self, unable to summon the courage to speak up, say what needs to be said and do what needs to be done.

Logically thinking through how you'll approach the unknown, handle the negative feedback or tackle the perceived threat will rebuild your confidence and ultimately your self-esteem. Given the subject of this book and the need to challenge a defective system and create a psychologically safe space in which to do the right thing, write down the answers to the following questions:

a) What specifically is it that you're worried/concerned/threatened by? (be as specific as you can)

b) What exactly do you think will happen if you do/say/challenge/tackle the above? (again, be as specific as you can)

c) Have you ever been in a similar situation yet managed to succeed despite your concerns? If so, write down what you remember about that situation.

d) Write down exactly what you did and how you felt afterwards.

e) Write down what the first small step is towards being BRAVE and doing/saying what needs to be done/said.

f) Write down what would stop you taking that first small step.

g) Write down what needs to be in place/happen and what's

within your control to help you take that first small step.

h) Write down any excuses you'll tell yourself that will stop you taking that first small step.

i) Write down your counterarguments to your excuses for the above.

Now answer the following in relation to your first small step action:

★ What will happen if I do/say this?
★ What will happen if I don't do/say this?
★ What won't happen if I do/say this?
★ What won't happen if I don't do/say this?

Now write down what emotions you feel when you think about doing/saying your first small step action.

Now write down what positive emotions you'll feel once you've successfully taken your first small step action.

Having carefully considered what may obstruct you from taking your first small step action and how you can overcome any internal barriers you may have created, you're ready to take that first step. As Susan Jeffers would say, sometimes you just need to feel the fear and do it anyway! (Jeffers 2012) So, open up your calendar, select a date and time, commit the action to your calendar – and to yourself! Tell others that you trust and respect and who'll be candid with you what you've committed to and by when. Ask them to hold you accountable for taking this action. Above all, be honest with yourself about making this action a reality.

Step 2: Develop your RESOLVE

Don't move on to step two until you've completed step one. This is important, as there's no point being persistent without courage and boldness. You'll simply persist in something that keeps you stuck where you are. However, once you've taken that first small step, you need to have the resolve to see things through to their conclusion. There will always be obstacles in your way, whether physical, the objections of others or, often, the obstacles you create in your own mind. As you've seen in Chapter 3, the human brain doesn't distinguish between something that's actually happening around you and what you're imagining is happening – ie the internal construct of your imagination. Your brain will react in the same way, creating the trigger for your emotional and behavioural reactions and responses. If you're lacking resilience and emotional intelligence and your emotional reaction is negative after your first attempt at your small step action, you're more likely to give up after that first attempt.

For those of you who have experienced your toddlers learning to walk, you'll know how awe inspiring it is to watch the persistence of these young minds. Uninhibited by internal dialogue, they'll use whatever is around to help them stand. They'll take that first bold step, physically releasing their grip on stability to step into the unknown – often with a smile on their face. The wobbling, the falling down, time and time again, never deters the determined youngster from achieving their goal. Remember, this was you once upon a time. You know exactly how to be persistent and develop the resolve you need to keep going in the face of challenges or threats.

Write down the answers to the following questions:

a) Think of a time when you gave up trying to do something after one or two attempts and write down your level of commitment from 1 (low) to 10 (high).

b) When you gave up, what emotions did you feel?

c) How long did these emotions last?

d) Now think of a time when you were relentless in the pursuit of your goal, you persisted and your resolve paid off. Write down your level of commitment from 1 (low) to 10 (high).

e) If your level of commitment is less than 8, write down what you need to do to reach at least a level 8 **for commitment to your first small step action**.

f) When your persistence has paid off in the past, what emotions did you feel?

g) Write down the successful vision of you achieving your first small step action (being as specific as possible).

h) Realistically, how many times will you need to attempt your first small step action before you succeed?

i) Write down the positive inner dialogue you'll say to yourself to keep yourself motivated each time you encounter an obstacle.

j) Write down your motivational direction (are you motivated *towards* achieving or gaining something such as a promotion or buying a new car, or are you motivated *away* from something such as not wanting to become unhealthy or not wanting to spend the next 20 years in the same role).

Now think about your level of self-discipline – the ability to do what you should be doing and stay on track. By developing self-discipline, you'll find it easier to overcome those negative emotions each time you fail to fully achieve your goals, vision or first small step action. Self-discipline enables you to tap into your emotional intelligence and rationalise each failure so that you can persist in your efforts. **DO NOT BE AFRAID OF FAILURE.** Failure is how we learn – you failed plenty of times when you were learning to walk. Fail faster, reflect on what went wrong, try again in a slightly different way – but **KEEP TRYING.** Remember, *practice makes permanent*, so make sure you learn what went wrong and next time do things differently. As you'll most certainly have heard, the modern definition of madness is doing the same thing over and over again and expecting a different result.

Step 3: Become AWARE and adaptable

How much do you really know yourself? If backed into a corner, how would you react? Would you respond differently if you were in your survival zone compared to your performance zone? What would the difference be? So often you'll fill in personality questionnaires, marvelling at how accurate the results are. But what's often missing from these tools is the 'so what?' factor. They're interesting but do you know what to do with the results? However, such tools can be extremely useful in the development of not just your self-awareness but also your ability to adapt your thinking and attitude as well as physical and emotional responses. Without this essential skill, you'll be unable to break free from the internal constraints you've placed around yourself, keeping you firmly stuck in your comfort zone.

We once worked with a highly influential yet domineering senior leader in a UK-based consumer goods company. He was intimidating and ruled by fear. He was highly aware of his personality traits and characteristics, how these shaped his responses and how they negatively impacted others. His bullying went unchallenged for years. Apart from demonstrating a high level of arrogance, what this tells you is that it's possible to be self-aware and consciously choose unhelpful, possibly damaging, behaviour. This unforgivable attitude can result in perpetual fear, pushing people to not only emotionally disengage from work but also become stressed, burnt out and deliberately destructive. Needless to say, psychological safety is impossible to achieve with behaviour such as this shaping the culture.

So why would a self-aware person deliberately choose *not* to adapt? Why would they relish creating such a fearful environment? Simple – they're unconsciously driven by fear themselves, fear of being exposed as a fraud or not good enough. The constant need to prove their intellect, skill, power or control is simply a cover-up for some deeper level of self-doubt. By making others appear inferior or by creating such an aura of fear, they remove the risk of being challenged or questioned which, in their minds, may result in exposure. In such minds, this is to be avoided at all costs, so instead of looking for ways to adapt thinking, attitude, feelings and behaviours, the offending behaviour is instead perfected to a fine art. Remember, practice makes permanent, meaning it becomes extremely difficult over time for such people to change their behaviour – unless they're in complete control of the situation.

Adapting means changing and that can feel scary, hence the need for bravery. *Change happens in an instant.* It's the point at which you stop doing one thing and start doing another. The build-up to change, however, can take a long time and involve huge amounts of internal wrangling, coupled with enormous amounts of emotional energy. Yet the benefits are so worthwhile. Adaptability is the key to the shackles binding you to old ways of thinking and responding. Once free from these restrictions you can give yourself permission to be the kind of person you know you are and to do the things you've been preventing yourself from doing. No longer will you be restricted by old thoughts or behaviour patterns. You'll develop the flexibility of mind needed to look at yourself, others and the world from different perspectives. Remember, *wisdom comes from multiple perspectives.*

Adapting your perception of others

Think of an individual that you struggle to interact positively with. Write down the answers to the following questions:

a) When you think of this person, what words immediately come to mind?
b) When you think of interacting with this person, what emotions do you feel?
c) What is it that this person does that you find challenging?

Remember, *perception is projection* – whatever you think of this person it will be unconsciously projected through your voice qualities (tone, pitch, cadence) and your body language (facial expression, tension in your muscles, gestures). It's through these unconscious signals that others can connect (or not) to you. If your unconscious signals come from a negative perception, even if unconsciously so, they will be received negatively. The resulting response will therefore be negative, creating a vicious cycle. This cycle needs to be broken and it starts with you adapting your perception of the individual.

Write down the answers to the following questions:

a) What is this person skilled at doing?
b) What positive qualities does this person have?
c) What do you most respect about them?

Prior to any interaction with this person, you'll need to focus on your positive answers – the individual's skills, positive qualities and aspects of them that you respect. It's important that your answers are genuine even if they may be, in your view, minor positives. By focusing on a positive, you'll change your mindset in that moment from negative to positive. This will ensure that your unconscious communication signals are positive, thus breaking the cycle of negativity.

By way of an example of how this exercise can work in practice, we worked for many years with a highly excitable and volatile client in a neighbouring European country. When not interacting face to face, communication was restricted to emails and phone calls. These calls tended to be quite fractious and frustrating on both sides. As time went by with more calls than face to face meetings, the frustration began to compound, exacerbated by the bluntness of the emails in between calls. Taking a logical, evidence-based approach with this client simply angered her more, exposing her to her own shortcomings – a naïve move on our part which fractured the relationship even further. However, always willing to reflect, learn from our own mistakes and try new ways of doing things, we used the exercise above. By this point, it was extremely difficult to find even the smallest of positives about this person. Racking our brains, we went over many details to the point of getting quite personal about her. We were both in agreement, however, that our client was extremely stylish and always impeccably turned out and her shoes were amazing! So, in preparation for our next face to face meeting, we focused on our belief that this person had fantastic taste in shoes. One of the first things we said to her when we next saw her was, 'Your shoes are amazing!' The effect was instantly disarming because, as we had previously, she'd been anticipating a difficult interaction, given the level of frustration that had built up prior to this meeting.

The lesson here is, no matter how minor a detail may seem to you, if it's genuinely positive, you can use this to focus on to adapt your perception in that moment. In terms of systems thinking, if you change one thing in the system – your perception – you'll change the whole system. This is because the response to your adapted perception will be different to the usual response to those unconscious negative communication signals that you may have been previously projecting. Remember, because communication signals are unconscious, they're not intentionally aimed at you – that would be considered a malicious act. However, when operating on autopilot, you often take those signals personally, based on your perception at that time – which is influenced by your current level of emotional intelligence and resilience.

Now once more, think of that person that you find it difficult to interact with. Write down the answers to the following questions:

a) What specifically has this person done that you find difficult to deal with?
b) How many times has this person done that behaviour in the past four weeks?
c) What emotions do you feel when this person does that behaviour?
d) How long do the negative emotions last?

Now go back to the positives about this person that you wrote down previously. Imagine two very different images:

1. An image of that person with all their positive qualities.
2. An image of their actual behaviour that you don't like.

This is the beginning of you being able to separate the person from their behaviour – a useful skill when learning to be BRAVE.

Psychologically, dealing with behaviour is much easier than dealing with a person and is much less damaging to that person.

Next, imagine you're living the life of that person, having to deal with all their day to day stresses and strains, challenges, difficulties, traumas and life events. Imagine what they must be experiencing on a daily basis. Importantly, imagine what it must feel like to be living their life and become curious about what might be driving their behaviour. Now think back to the emotional quadrants model – what quadrant do you think they're spending most of their time in? Remember that being stuck in either of the negative quadrants will impact how you respond to people, situations and life in general.

Start developing a real sense of the human being behind the behaviour that you see from that person. It takes bravery to set aside your prior negative perception of someone and truly accept the human being. However, remember that most of the behaviour you find challenging is likely to be unconscious and not deliberately aimed at you. Given the challenges in that person's life that you've just imagined, you should now be able to choose whether to hold on to your negative perception or adapt it, given a deeper understanding of that person and your ability to empathise with another human being.

The easier, less emotionally intelligent option is to continue to hold on to your negative perception, generalising negatively about that individual with thoughts such as:

* every time she does *x*
* he's a walking disaster
* every time I see her she does *y*
* every time I have to speak to him there's trouble
* she never does what I ask
* he's never on time
* everything she does is useless
* he's always been the same, he'll never change.

It's these types of thoughts that will project your negativity, keeping the negative spiral on its downward journey. The same will, of course, apply to the collective, ie the organisation you work for or a team you work with.

To avoid the trap of continually generalising about another person negatively, you need to challenge your perception of that person. Write down the answers to the following questions, relating to the same individual you've used for the previous exercises as your example (being as specific as possible):

a) When did this person *not* exhibit the challenging behaviour and what was the difference (for example, was the interaction easier or more productive)?

b) How long ago did this person exhibit more positive behaviour?

c) Out of ten interactions with this person, how many times does this person exhibit more positive behaviour?

d) Thinking of yourself, is there more to you than the limited amount of behaviour that people see from you in one context, for example, work?

e) If this is true of yourself, could this be true of the person you find challenging to deal with? Is there more to them than just the challenging behaviour you experience from them in a very limited context, such as work?

f) If (d) and (e) above are true, what does this mean for:
   – your perception of this person?
   – your future interactions with this person?
   – your perception of yourself?

These answers are building the evidence bank you need to challenge your perspective of that person. That's not to say that you shouldn't challenge the behaviour in question – this is a must and needs to be addressed. Here, you need to gather evidence **to give feedback on specific instances of the behaviour** – not as a generalisation about the individual at an identity level. Such behaviour should be called out in a matter of fact way, without you becoming angry, defensive or upset. Simply state specifically what the behaviour is that you find inappropriate, when that behaviour occurred, why it's inappropriate and what your expectations are going forward.

For many people, giving feedback isn't an easy thing to do and is often related to fear and anxiety that has manifested in anticipation of a negative response to the feedback. This is where you need to dig deep into your inner strength. The more you can step out of your comfort zone, the more you'll be increasing your strength of character. By pushing yourself to have the difficult conversations, you're demonstrating your bravery. Utilising your knowledge of different personality types and adapting your own communication style will ease the feedback pathway.

Of course, practising how to change your perception of others also goes a long way towards helping you to change your perception of yourself. This is much more important if you're struggling to see yourself as a courageous person.

So start with your perception of other people first. Practise changing your perception of them. Once this becomes easier, then go on to the exercises for changing your perception of yourself. If you're struggling, see yourself initially in the third person, imagining you're just another person.

Adapting your self-perception

If you don't already see yourself as a brave person, then adapting your self-perception is crucial. Even if you don't feel very brave yet, it's important to start building a picture of yourself as a brave person. To start this process, write down the answers to the following questions:

a) What do you currently think about yourself? Be as specific as possible – capture any actual internal thoughts, beliefs, feelings.
b) When you read this back, what emotions does it evoke?
c) If these emotions are negative, how long are you likely to feel them?
d) How would you *like* others to see you? Be as specific as possible – use positive words or statements that you'd like others to use to describe you.
e) When you read this back, what emotions does it evoke?

f) Write down the evidence others might use to base their positive perception of you on.

g) When you're having your best, most resilient, emotionally intelligent, BRAVE day ever, write down the answer to the following questions:
   – How do you deal with setbacks?
   – How do you deal with criticism?
   – How do you deal with change?
   – How do you support others?
   – How do you look after yourself?

h) Think of a specific time in your life when you were really proud of yourself or your achievements. Write down how you felt about yourself at that moment. Be as specific and positive as possible.

Complete the following using positive language only:

★ I am capable of achieving...
★ From today, I will commit to making the following changes...
★ Even if my plans don't go as I'd hoped, I will still be...

The above answers are your foundation for adapting and *reframing* your self-perception. Re-read your answers and then rewrite your new positive self-perception, starting with *I am...*

Now write down what your first three steps will be to move you towards stepping into your new brave self.

Write down any potential barriers to you taking these first three steps and how you'll overcome those barriers, remembering that one of the biggest barriers may be your own internal dialogue and limiting beliefs.

Remember, whatever your self-perception, you'll still give off unconscious communication signals to others that reflect your perception of yourself. As an example, think back to Chapter 6 and the Karpman drama triangle. If you perceive yourself to be any of these three characters – persecutor, victim or rescuer – you'll project that image onto others and this is how they'll perceive you and respond to you. It's only at the point of adapting your self-perception that you can step out of the drama triangle and associated roles to take a more emotionally intelligent approach to responding to the situation you find yourself in. If you can develop your self-perception as being a brave person, you'll be better equipped to deal with life's ups and downs.

Adapting your perception of situations

It's not just your self-perception nor your perception of others that can affect your ability to be brave. Situations, or more accurately, your negative perception of situations, can be just as debilitating. This is because your negative perception of yourself locks you into patterns of unhelpful behaviour and stops you intentionally climbing out of your comfort zone in order to do things differently. Particularly in the workplace, people often perceive that they should or shouldn't do or say things for fear of negative consequences, thus holding themselves back, not saying or doing what really needs to be said or done. Over time, this squashing of our sense of what's right and just can ultimately damage our confidence and sense of self-value, remembering that everyone has a fundamental need to feel valued.

Such situations often arise due to the unspoken rules or beliefs created within the subcultures that we're subject to. The 'this is just the way it is' belief can keep you locked in a cycle of compliance despite knowing that what you're doing is actually the wrong thing to do. Yet the fear of negative consequences if you don't comply can be so powerful, it will frequently hinder your urge to do the right thing or do anything at all.

As Viktor Frankl said, we are 'a result of the decisions we make, not the environment we find ourselves in'. Therefore how you adapt your perception and response to the situations you find yourself in will be a key factor in successfully embracing your brave self. Your brave self can see situations for what they are, without allowing your negative emotions to trample your desire to do things differently or step into the unknown.

To break free of the negative emotional grip you may be in, think of a situation that you know you will at some point have to face and that you're dreading. Write down the answers to the following questions:

a) Describe the situation in as much detail as possible.
b) When you think of this situation, what emotions does it evoke?
c) How intense are these emotions? (1 = low, 10 = high)
d) What would success look like if you were to deal with this situation in a positive way? (be as specific as possible)
e) If you were to deal with this situation positively, what emotions would you feel?

Now undertake the following exercise. In your mind, create a movie clip of you dealing with this situation positively and successfully, making sure that you can see and hear yourself in the clip. Make it sharp, bright and colourful. Make sure that you can see your entire body in this clip, taking positive, successful actions. Make sure you can hear your own voice and that it sounds positive. Make the voices of those around you positive in their response to you. Make the clip as detailed as possible, from the beginning of the situation all the way to the end where you successfully deal with the situation and overcome any obstacles you may encounter along the way.

Next, imagine you're sitting in a cinema looking up at the big screen. You're alone, feeling safe and comfortable. Your movie clip is playing on the big screen. Follow these steps:

1. Watch your movie clip all the way through from beginning to end, making sure you can see and hear yourself in the clip.
2. When you get to the end, rewind back to the beginning of the clip.
3. Now imagine stepping inside of your own body within

that movie clip (so you can see your own hands as you look at them, but not your face as you're now experiencing being inside your own body in the movie), as you now take the actions you just watched yourself do.

4. Now that you are imagining being inside your own body, begin to feel and hear yourself taking all those positive actions as you run the movie clip through to its successful conclusion. Importantly, ensure you feel the positive emotions related to your clip.

5. When you get to the end of the clip, imagine stepping back into your seat in the cinema, so once again you are looking at yourself within the movie clip.

6. Rewind the movie clip back to the beginning and watch it all over again from beginning to end, ensuring you can see yourself in the clip.

7. Repeat steps three to six above, at least ten times.

Usually, due to the existing neurological pathways in your brain, whenever you think about that perceived negative situation, you'll strengthen those pathways. This means it becomes quicker, almost instantaneous, for your brain to think of the situation and feel negative – boom! Just like that, you feel negative. This exercise will do two things. First, it causes confusion in your brain, making it more difficult for that negative feeling to manifest. Second, the exercise creates new, fresher, stronger – and importantly – positive neurological pathways. By mentally rehearsing how you'll successfully deal with the situation and repeating the exercise at least ten times in quick succession, these new neurological pathways will dominate over the old negative ones. This powerful exercise is extremely useful in helping you significantly reduce and even eliminate any fear and anxiety you may be feeling towards that situation. You can use the exercise to adapt how you deal with any event or situation that you're concerned about.

Step 4: Act VIRTUOUSLY

Our deeply held values help guide us through life, determining what's right and wrong, meriting what's of importance or of worth, and what we regard as being deserved. However, values without action are simply aspirations. A virtue is a value in action. Virtues are the enablers of striving for certain ideals such as dedication, excellence or doing what's right for the common good. You can discover your ideals through thoughtful reflection on what you see as your potential – visualising the kind of person you want to be.

Take some time to think about and reflect on the above, ie what kind of person you want to be. Write down a detailed description of your ideal self.

Virtues are attitudes, character traits and dispositions that enable you to act in ways that develop and fulfil your potential. Examples are courage, compassion, fairness, self-regulation and integrity.

Write down your top three virtues that you want to live your life by. Then, next to each of your three virtues, rate each one of them (1 = low, 10 = high) in terms of the need for development, for example, integrity = 8, if you struggle with it and have a high need to develop it; or honesty = 3, if it comes naturally to you and is, therefore, a low need for development.

According to the Markkula Center for Applied Ethics, virtues can be developed through learning about yourself, your mistakes and practice (see Velasquez et al 1988 and scu.edu/ethics/ethics-resources). You'll recollect that practice makes permanent; therefore practice must come as the result of reflection and learning. Aristotle suggested that you can improve your character through self-discipline, yet corrupt your *good* character through repeated self-indulgence. Such indulgence could be giving in to complacency and acceptance, leading to inaction because you haven't yet developed the courage you need to act. Just like the ability to run a marathon is developed through training and practice, so too is your ability to act with integrity and your capacity to be courageous, fair and compassionate.

For each virtue above, write down what you need to practise to keep developing that virtue; for example, 'Fairness – I will assess each person's related decision from multiple perspectives and check with my own gut feeling that my decision feels fair.'

Once acquired, virtues develop into characteristics as they become habitually ingrained in how you live your life. They become part of how others see you and part of your identity. For example, if you develop the virtue of compassion, you're likely to be referred to as a compassionate person. This in turn is likely to lead you to be naturally disposed to act in ways that are consistent with your moral principles because a virtuous person is an ethical person. We know this can be challenging as even in our consulting work our own virtues of integrity, honesty, fairness and self-control are regularly put to the test. Challenging circumstances sometimes mean we have to make tough decisions in order to stay aligned with who we are as people and who we are as consultants, and consider our professional integrity and our sense of fairness both to ourselves and our clients.

One of our clients recently asked us to create a training intervention for them from the ground up. No specific brief was given regarding the content or who would be delivering it. The only specific constraint was the length of time the intervention should take to deliver. Open goals like this are great and there would naturally be plenty of scope for trying out different approaches with creative experimentation and candid feedback going in both directions. Given our shared enthusiasm for the subject matter, it was taken as read that the project represented a psychologically safe space in which to experiment, be open and candid, without fear of negative consequences. As it turned out, we found ourselves in the exact opposite position. Getting agreement on the content and format of the intervention took longer than planned (with delays on both sides), resulting in the project taking much longer than anticipated. We knew challenging the client's blaming behaviour toward us would be risky; we knew holding our boundaries would be risky; we knew holding others accountable would be risky. However, we also knew that failure to do so would mean we were hypocrites, saying we believed in one thing yet behaving in a non-congruent way. We wouldn't be able to hold our heads up as professionals acting with integrity. Given that our values are the cornerstone of our consulting practice, we had little choice but to be open about the impact of their behaviour towards us. The result was extremely painful: we were dropped from the project.

At this point you might think the risk wasn't worth it and that if you'd been in this position you'd have kept quiet. Trust us when we say we had the same wavering thought. However, we decided to dig deep into our inner strength and were courageous enough to do what we felt to be the right thing, even though we knew that in the short term it could affect us financially – which it did. We weren't reckless in our decision to seek fair treatment from our client and challenge their behaviour. We had to do a lot of reflection on who we wanted to be as a consultancy to get to that point. But we had to place a value on our self-worth and knew, regardless of the outcome, that we'd still be OK. In fact, we'd be more than OK because we'd emerge from the difficulty stronger and with more conviction than ever before. We were consciously our authentic selves in that moment, compassionate towards others who weren't quite where we were, and knew that in the final analysis, sticking to our values is what pays the real dividends.

You can see from this example the importance of acting virtuously and with authenticity. Being BRAVE means you must know who you are and act in accordance with your values, virtues and authenticity. Any hint of disingenuousness will be immediately recognisable impacting you, your outlook and how others see you. It's by no means easy to do this. You need to draw on all factors that make you a brave person to really understand how your virtues form the inner core of your strength of character. The factors in the BRAVE model don't operate in isolation, they're symbiotically linked. Therefore the final step is equally as important as the previous four.

Step 5: Critically EVALUATE evidence

Being BRAVE doesn't equate to being reckless. Recklessness would be deliberately acting in a way that consciously disregards the risks or consequences such action poses. To critically evaluate means to understand your judgements may vary from different perspectives, with some judgements being stronger than others. It requires you to be analytical, objective and develop reasoned arguments for your judgements based on your ability to adapt and see situations from multiple perspectives – not just your own immediate perspective. This will enable you to take calculated risks – just as we did in our example above. We carefully considered the consequences of our actions and drew upon our own strength of character to help us make a very difficult decision. We demonstrated our emotional maturity and did the right thing, knowing that the outcome in the near term wouldn't be favourable. However, we were also able to see the bigger picture and the long-term vision we had for ourselves and our consultancy – short-term pain for hopefully long-term gain, with a huge dollop of self-respect and credibility along the way. Such brave decisions are never easy. In fact, they're extremely difficult and often painful, which is why it's essential for you to critically evaluate the situation from a variety of perspectives.

Thinking of a decision or course of action you need to take, write down five alternatives to your decision, including your reasoning for each option.

Now rank each option in terms of how easy or difficult it would be for you to carry out (1 = very easy, 10 = very difficult).

Check in with yourself – are you drawn to taking one of the easier options? Remember, human beings are wired to take the path of least resistance – the easiest path, which may not be the best path. Write down what evidence you have to support a favourable outcome for each option.

Next, write down the assumptions you're making for each option and what would happen if these assumptions were incorrect:

Finally, go back over your answers for each option and then write an argument for each one, as if you were trying to convince your boss of your decision.

Once you've developed the ability to critically evaluate, you can then decide on the wisest course of action. This is when you need to think through the consequences of your decisions or choices – looking at how these may play out in the bigger picture. Before making your final decision or choice, ask yourself:

a. How will this reflect on me?
b. How will this reflect on my team?
c. How will this reflect on my performance?
d. Is this something I can be proud of?
e. Am I making a decision from the best version of myself, in my performance zone (see Chapter 6)?

You may need to slow down your response just a little bit so you can decide on the wisest course of action. Write down the answers to the following questions:

a. Who is the wisest person you know?
b. What would they do in this situation?
c. What would they *not* do in this situation?
d. What barriers are stopping *me* from making a similar decision?
e. How can I overcome these barriers?

Now you're at the stage of being able to make your choice, having carefully considered the alternatives, structured your reasoning, evaluated the evidence and developed your argument. Bring all this together to form how you'd communicate your decision:

My decision/choice is...
and the rationale for my choice is...

On a scale of 1 = low to 10 = high, how positive do you feel about your decision?

If not a 10, is there anything you can do to move that feeling closer to a 10? If so, write down what that is.

If you're still not convinced about your choice, write down the answers to these questions (first introduced earlier in this chapter):

    a. What will happen if I do this?
    b. What will happen if I don't do this?
    c. What won't happen if I do this?
    d. What won't happen if I don't do this?

Critical evaluation takes practice, especially as it requires taking a long, hard look at the alternatives, in the context of you being a brave person. Evaluation is never done in isolation but symbiotically with the other factors of the model – boldness, resolve, adaptability and virtuousness. Only when you can critically evaluate within the context of the entire BRAVE model can you truly act wisely.

What does your BRAVE new world look like?

There's no doubt that the world of work and in particular the worker–employer relationship has been disrupted. Deloitte has scenario-planned some interesting future alternatives such as 'work as fashion', a reactive worker–employer relationship with employers feeling compelled to respond to immediate worker demands and competitor moves, with little or no connection to a sustainable workforce strategy. Or 'work is work', whereby organisational responsibility and personal/social fulfilment are seen as separate domains and workers find purpose outside of work, with the worker–employer relationship being professional. Or 'purpose unleashed', whereby a sense of purpose drives the working relationship between workers and employers with a communal relationship and shared purpose binding them together (Schwartz et al 2021).

Whatever the future may hold for organisations and their workers, the future will be different from the traditional *survival* mindset following an economic crisis. The assumption, or hope, that the world will revert to normal once the external pressure dissipates has seen many organisations treading water with short-term strategies to navigate the future. Unfortunately, such strategies do not bode well for long-term success. To truly thrive under pressure, workers and employers need to recognise that disruption is continuous and needs to be embraced to keep moving forward. Taking those brave leaps may seem unconventional or aspirational to those lacking the same level of bravery. Yet those brave ideas and practices could catapult the ability to unlock workforce potential and new perspectives. The good news is that you now have the tools to develop your own ability to tackle those disruptions – maybe even create your own. What possibilities could arise, what doors would open, what could be achieved? More importantly, what do you *want* to be different?

Our political and socioeconomic agenda is not about bashing capitalism; however, it is about raising the question of ethically making money – being successful without destroying workers along the way. It's about being someone who can authentically feel they work or lead in a way that embraces personal wealth, health and success, alongside the wealth, health and success of others – not at the expense of it. It's about the move away from shareholder value at all costs because, according to the *Harvard Business Review*, people want to be part of something that's bigger than themselves (Goffee & Jones 2013). People want to believe in what their organisation stands for, with a shared meaning that forges and maintains a powerful connection between workers and organisational values. This fosters both individuality and simultaneously a compelling culture about *how* you do business.

Think back to when most life insurance companies were demutualising and becoming financial services supermarkets; New York Life rejected this trend, insisting that as they were so good at life insurance it would remain their core focus. It was more than a simple business strategy; it was their everyday way of operating, where values flew in the face of trying to wriggle out of paying claims. One customer took out a life insurance policy, went home and wrote out the cheque but died that same night. The policy hadn't been paid for, yet New York Life paid the claim. The employees truly bought into this culture and its values.

And then there's Rabobank Nederland, which rolled out Rabo Unplugged – an organisational and technical infrastructure enabling employees to connect to one another from practically anywhere while still meeting the stringent encryption standards required by the banking industry. It has no fixed offices or job descriptions and employees are free to choose how, where, when and with whom they work. This approach requires an extraordinary amount of trust by managers as well as demanding that employees are more entrepreneurial and collaborative.

We've witnessed some amazing feats of human effort, inspiration and compassion, none more so than during the global Covid-19 pandemic. These acts demonstrate how human beings have an inordinate ability to pull together, do the right thing and be compassionate towards one another. For example, Aimee Karam from Lebanon was part of a fundraising campaign to support the disadvantaged that saw $1 million raised in one hour on the first day of fundraising. She ascribed this success to the shared values of transparency, political independence, integrity and non-discrimination. Captain Tom Moore is another remarkable example of human determination who, at the age of 99, began his own fundraising campaign in aid of the UK's National Health Service by walking 100 lengths of his garden. In total he raised a staggering £32.79 million. Greek entrepreneur Melina Taprantzi lived through the Greek financial crisis and pandemic. Her business, Wise Greece, connects small-scale food producers with those in need such as the vulnerable and elderly who can't leave their homes by providing 6 kg food and supply boxes, distributing more than 50 tonnes of food supplies since 2013, with 6 tonnes alone during the pandemic. The global shortage of sanitising products during the pandemic saw Chad's government officials and scientists come together in record time to launch the country's first ever local manufacturer of hand sanitiser, producing 900 litres per day.

These are just a few of the many amazing stories of human beings pulling out all the stops, collaborating, being virtuous and resilient. Your story doesn't have to be on such a grand scale but it should evoke feelings of pride. You may have been continually trying to put out that fire that burns inside you, that really wants to be brave and do something, in *your* view, remarkable. It's your view that counts, so don't compare yourself to others or to the actions and achievements of others. They're not you and that's great! The challenge in being brave is to create a psychologically safe environment where individuality, collaboration and candidness are nurtured – all for the greater good. To avoid overinflated egos, harsh or hurtful feedback or polite talking shops, there needs to be discussion and agreement about how they will work in practice.

Never has there been such a golden opportunity to fan those flames and allow that fire to grow, pushing you into the action you've previously held in check. Go back over the answers to the questions above in this chapter. Remind yourself of your positive qualities, your authentic self, your small step actions, your evidence to act – all the things you've written that will convince you that you're brave enough to write your new story.

Write down the answers to the following:

* ★ The old me held me back from doing...
* ★ and being...
* ★ Now I am...
* ★ and I will...
* ★ This will help me because...
* ★ My personal mission is...
* ★ This will make me feel...
* ★ I will hold myself accountable by...
* ★ To support me, I can call upon...
* ★ I will manage my setbacks by...

It's not easy doing the right thing, being true to yourself, stepping into your BRAVE self, especially as most people don't always live and work in a psychologically safe world. However, that shouldn't stop you being who you want to be. Be wary of fads and fashions that sweep the corporate world. Challenging the new initiative or even the status quo, putting yourself out there and doing things differently are all risky. Yet without taking risks, you'll never grow, develop new strengths and magnify your existing strengths. Be clear about what you do well but remember, if you never grow, eventually you'll stagnate. So be brave and take those calculated risks. Learn from your failures. Try again, in a different way. Be clear about who you are and what you stand for. Above all, be bold and courageous – be brave!

Chapter 7: Big questions

- ★ If you're a **team member**: what behaviours demonstrate how you live and breathe your internal values?
- ★ If you're a **people leader**: how do you demonstrate authenticity as the manager of your team?
- ★ If you're a **senior leader**: what is the brave challenge that you need to set for yourself as a leader of your organisation?

Key messages

- ★ Authenticity is the foundation for developing congruence, feeling comfortable in your own skin and in the decisions you make. Authenticity is the demonstration of your deeply held values and the way you live your life, manage your people and lead your company.
- ★ To be BRAVE requires a high degree of self-awareness and the strength of character to develop your aptitude to be bold, have resolve, adapt your perception, act virtuously and evaluate situations before making decisions.
- ★ Being BRAVE unlocks your potential for innovation and creativity, to disrupt the norm, take calculated risks and step into the best version of yourself, acknowledging your limitations and accepting yourself for who you are.

8 BRAVE from a safe space

So are you all set? You've done the groundwork to provide the foundation for a culture that feels generally safe, leadership are modelling the right behaviours and letting people know they don't have *all* the answers and everyone knows their roles and responsibilities in relation to keeping the culture free of fear. People are also feeling confident that there won't be any negative consequences as a result of practising self-care by prioritising their wellbeing and managing their personal resources in a sustainable way. You've also absorbed the lessons of Chapters 6 and 7 and are now personally resilient and brave. Now that all the pieces are in place, you just need to ask the questions and unbridled feedback and invaluable insights will now flow freely.

Well, almost but not quite. The trouble with fear is that it hangs around, mainly due to an ancestral survival preference for remembering negative experiences over positive ones. As demonstrated by the stress statistics, people have become accustomed to not necessarily telling it how it really is. Instead they find ways of ploughing on and coping, even when it comes at the expense of their wellbeing and personal sustainability. All habits take time to break, including cognitive ones. There will be a period where people look for observable changes in others, to provide the reassurance they need before they update their interpersonal risk assessment criteria and decide to behave differently. They also haven't read this book, of course, so they also won't know what you know about strength of character and bravery and the change agent potential of them both. They'll be waiting for cues from others that it's safe to speak up.

The obvious issue with this is that if everybody waits for everyone else – and nobody wants to be the first to go – progress can be non-existent. To speed things up, there's one more important step you can take, and that's to create safe spaces for teams to talk. They need to be specific to this purpose, not tacked on to the end of another meeting, and structured to encourage open conversations between colleagues. Opportunities such as these can create the right conditions in which to share insights, deepen trust and discover fresh perspectives. The manager's role is to offer a psychologically safe space for ideation and openness, holding the space but not driving the agenda – inviting and harvesting employee ideas, experiences and shared insights for the team to explore with each other. These are safe, custom spaces created for the sole purpose of ring-fencing time to catalyse openness and support a fear-free approach to problem solving and collaboration.

Safe, in this context, means that everyone involved knows there are no right or wrong answers and they're there to share their perspective openly and honestly. The purpose of the exercise is to open up to the viewpoints of others and practise curiosity about how this or that insight might update or develop current thinking. When dedicated time is specifically allocated to this type of discussion, the people involved start to shed their concerns about negative personal consequences resulting from sharing novel or individual viewpoints. It also becomes much more obvious how they might directly contribute to a culture shift and what their role is going to be in maintaining a higher level of psychological safety for themselves and others.

It also means safe in the context of the interaction and dialogue being containable and controllable. Allocating specific time to a semi-structured discussion with the pre-communicated objective of hearing each other's views offers a space-holding framework from which to generate fresh insights but without dictating the content or pre-defining the outcome. It's a little like coming off the 'honey pot' footpath and striking off into more dense woodland, not quite knowing what you might come across but feeling OK because you have a compass and a map.

In these psychologically safe, semi-structured forums, team members can explore together how 'good' the work and the way they're doing it feel right now. They can examine the way they tend to respond to work challenges and why they respond that way. They can ask themselves what internal narratives they're all working to and whether, now that the world has changed, those stories could be reviewed and updated. They can identify what response behaviours work well for them right now and how these behaviours contribute to team energy and strengths. They can strategise how to maintain these behaviours when the pressure is on so that they don't lose the foundational benefits they bring. They can identify common pressure sources, unpack them properly and find areas where they can either moderate the pressure at source or change their response to it. They can assess the current level of team energy and honestly appraise how intentional they are, individually and collectively, about directing and renewing that energy so that it can produce the right return, sustainably. Most importantly they can openly explore ways in which they might be able to be the change they want to see and shape the way work is done for the best wellbeing and performance outcome.

Reimagining the now

The first chapter looked at the way in which private narratives shape how we think, feel and behave. We started the book with this theme because understanding internal storytelling is an important first step in taking the much needed primary prevention approach to improving wellbeing at work. In the safe spaces just described, conversations can go in one of two directions – addressing identified pressure at source (obviously the preferred option) or adapting the employee response to limit damage and make high performance healthy and sustainable. Both options require everyone involved to be able to recognise entrenched thinking and related behaviours and let go of limiting stories and beliefs about what might be possible.

The Walt Disney Corporation famously used the term 'imagineering' to describe the creative process of fully envisaging a theme park ride experience before making any attempt to mechanically engineer it. Dedicated and structured opportunities for focused and psychologically safe conversations, like the ones just detailed, direct teams and leaders to the parts of the team ride that might need recalibration. Because the process is employee centric and the detail is generated by the people 'at the coalface', employee-led blueprints to make these recalibrations happen are drawn up as part of the discussion. There's no need to sell the ideas back to possibly unwilling 'champions'. The investigation effectively generates its own energy to fuel targeted and meaningful team-led intervention.

Much of our work with corporate clients involves unlocking the insight capital hidden inside every employee which, without the right culture and mechanism through which to volunteer it, tends to stay right there. We do this by the method just described, enabling teams to lead their own discussions, often navigating by reference to a light-touch snapshot of their team energy and resilience starting point that everyone involved contributes to ahead of the session. Of course, you don't have to use an assessment tool to catalyse conversation but there's safety in anonymity, particularly when the process is new and unfamiliar. Individual trust and confidence take a while to build and everyone's starting in a different place, so anonymous, team-based orientation data can be really useful.

Assessment tools such as the ones we've developed for our own practice enable teams to identify and get going on the real issue almost immediately. In less than ten minutes they can get a picture of the sources of pressure that most impact them, how much energy they have and whether this is depleting or expanding. They can also see how well they're able to direct and renew their energy as a group, how psychologically safe they feel around each other and how aligned they feel with the team mission and purpose. They can even get a measure of whether pressure is producing stretch or strain outcomes for them. This information obviously helps them to direct their conversation towards the hottest topics, which saves time but critically also provides the baseline against which the team and their leadership can evaluate progress in the near future.

Not a 'one day only' opportunity

Figure 1 below shows the flow of the approach that we've just been describing and which many clients have now built into their wellbeing offering. All our tools offer participants personal confidential feedback, so many clients use the tools in two simultaneous ways. The availability of the individual report enables clients to genuinely position the assessment as a personal wellbeing management tool. This provides an opportunity to receive a confidential snapshot of their individual energy and resilience, the behaviours that are working for them and the ones that they might want to work on. Offering the assessment to individuals is also a means of signposting employees to the wellbeing learning and support services that their responses suggest are relevant. This can be a valuable way to connect the 'right' employees to the right support rather than hoping they'll find it when they need it.

Phase 1 Assessment	Phase 1 Group Report	Phase 2 Manager Coaching	Phase 3 Team Review	Phase 3 Action Planning	Phase 5 Follow-up
Team to complete the Team Energy Assessment and receive personal profiles	Anonymised team responses are sent to each nominated manager or team leader	1:1 session with internal resources to discuss results and plan for team meeting	Team and Manager review the group results together	Team collectively decide which issues are most important to them and agree action points. Manager supports.	Process is repeated to measure changes that have taken place since previous assessment

Figure 1: Team agility process

When the assessment tools are offered to intact teams the benefits just detailed apply but there's the additional benefit of offering the opportunity to understand *team* energy and resilience and thus stimulate the conversations detailed previously. Positioning of the assessment tool varies, depending on how the client wants to align this important part of their wellbeing strategy with other initiatives. Some refer to it as Team Agility, some Team Energy and some Team MOT.

Whatever the label, the process is the same, which is to get people into a psychologically safe space to share ideas, identify and celebrate the enablers and understand where their pressure comes from so they can work with their leaders to respond to it in fresh ways.

- ★ **Phase 1**: Pre-work involving a light-touch qualitative or quantitative assessment of team hot spots to guide the discussion and, in the case of quantitative assessment, provide a baseline against which to evaluate progress next time.
- ★ **Phase 2**: An opportunity for the manager to talk through the findings with a colleague (or consultant, if external support is involved) to sense-check them and establish a structure and waypoints for the discussion with the team.
- ★ **Phase 3**: Where the magic happens. Team and manager review together and explore how good the work is – how it feels to be part of this team right now – and unpack established responses. They celebrate and recommit to what they do well, challenge old stories and agree small step adaptations to work and wellbeing habits as required.
- ★ **Phase 4:** Repeat of Phase 1 after a few months to measure progress, see what's working and reset behind new or emerging priorities.

Repeated regularly, these types of conversations provide an easy way to address the sources of poor wellbeing at work and do so in the employee-centric way that's now necessary. By dedicating this space and time and creating space for people to speak up candidly, companies can actively demonstrate the value they claim to place on their employees. Formalising these opportunities is an easy way to demonstrate the value placed on their unique insights and in so doing push psychological safety up another notch.

As confidence in this safety expands across the business, the quantity and quality of insight improve proportionately. People lift the self-imposed barrier of fear, take higher level interpersonal risks and share more of what they know without fear of reprisal. Time ritually dedicated to this type of dialogue sends the most important message of all – that you're employed as a human being and are valued as a diverse and unique individual rather than a unit of production.

A global fast-moving consumer goods client, now on their fifth cycle of exploration, action and evaluation of progress, said recently that the process has been 'one of the great enablers for psychological safety in our team'. It's always great to receive feedback like this and the enthusiasm their leader has shown for the process speaks for itself but the progress they've made as a team is clearly visible in their data as well. Every six months or so they use a dedicated Team MOT session to check in with each other and explore their key sources of work pressure as a group. They look closely at the way they're using and recovering personal and collective energy and examine together whether their ways of working and self-care habits are amplifying or moderating the way their workplace pressures are experienced (Figure 2).

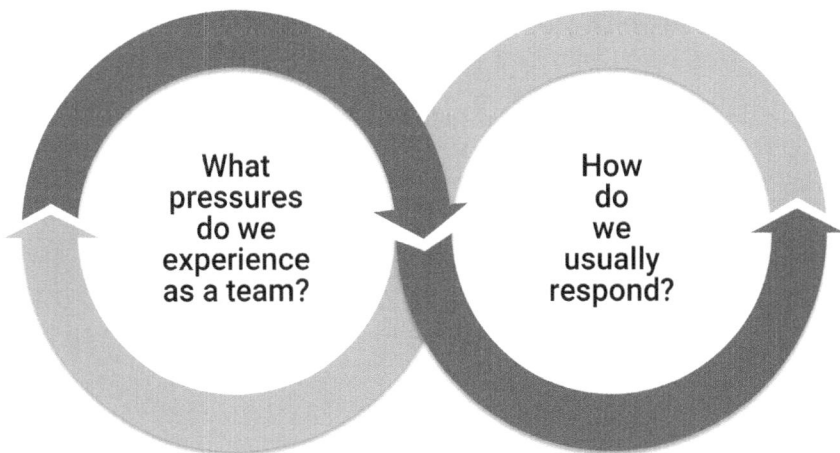

Figure 2: Pressure and response

What does it feel like to work here?

Like every team, everywhere, time and energy are at a premium and the reason they feel it has helped them so much is that their assessment data enables them to have open but focused conversations about the areas that affect them the most. Their objective each time is to identify small and specific behaviours or process adaptations that they can initiate for themselves which will incrementally improve team performance by making better use of energy resources. In this way they're able to maintain their status as a high-performing team while also improving wellbeing and avoiding burnout.

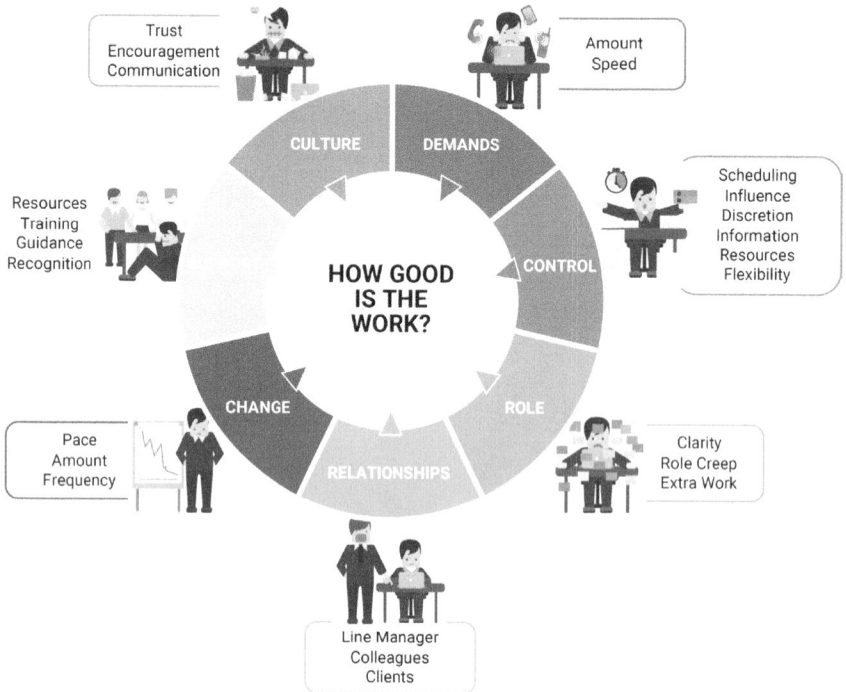

Figure 3: How good is the work?

In under an hour they can review how much pressure they feel in each of the areas identified in the diagram above. All of these are known drivers of workplace stress but ironically, and not unlike

Goldilocks' porridge, when they're 'just right' for people they're also the source of employee satisfaction and engagement. With knowledge of these sources of pressure in mind the team then assess whether they can be influenced in any way upstream or, if not, how they might adjust their responses to get the best wellbeing and performance outcome.

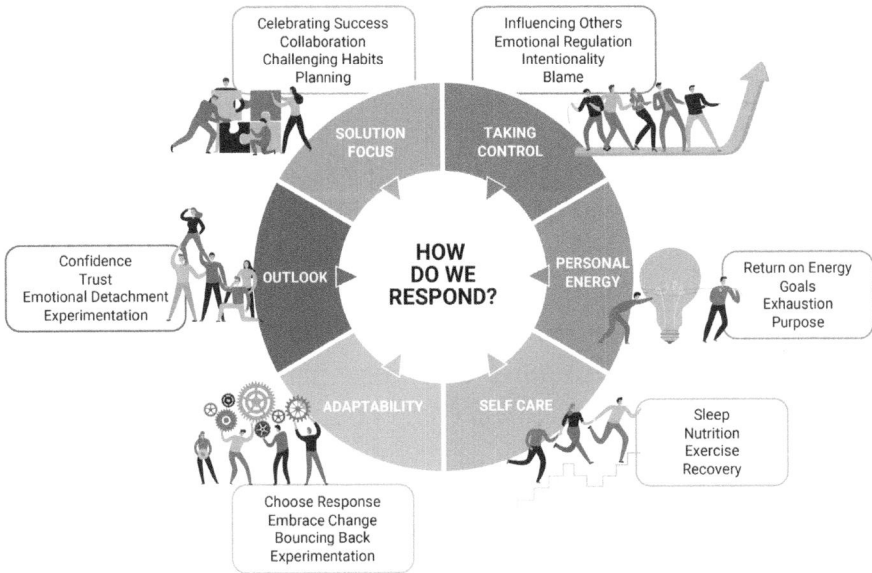

Figure 4: Factors in the response that affect the way work feels

Conversation flows continuously between looking for ways to moderate the pressure through challenging old habits, redundant processes and the entrenched ways of thinking that support them both (Figure 3) and how to build energy and adapt reactions to use that individual and collective energy to the best wellbeing effect (Figure 4).

Simply inclusive

Sometimes the simplest approaches work the best. For many employees, just being given the opportunity to share their experience, what works for them and what they feel could work better is all it takes to improve wellbeing. Others, as has been said, may have reasons to be nervous or sceptical about pushback or negative consequences so they'll hang back a bit as a result. But

195

that's OK. When they see others being bold with opinions regularly, with no resulting negative outcome, most will try out their voice a little more. This is how inclusion becomes real for people — there's no hidden agenda, and all you need to do is show up with your voice and be prepared to use it.

They're just like me!

Our workshop experience shows us that when people do take a breath and share their individual experiences and thoughts, something surprising happens – at least to them, if not to us. People quickly find out that what they previously might have viewed as an individual quirk of theirs, a private bugbear, pet peeve, solo frustration or just a personal weakness is not so unique to them after all. It seems that plenty of other team members have the same feelings. Even more revelatory is the discovery that their managers share the same emotions and have similar frustrations. Once people start dropping the work mask, it becomes clear that the sources of joy, satisfaction and workplace engagement (and their opposites) are more universal than people may have thought. As any leader knows, a more lofty place in the hierarchy is absolutely no guarantee of immunity from daily hassles, worry and fear. Sharing individual perspectives therefore often reveals unexpected commonality between people, fuelling empathy and connection. Who knew? Turns out your colleagues and managers might be more like you than you gave them credit for!

Personal power

When people feel that they have some agency, even if it's only in limited ways, then they feel empowered. The arbiter of whether work pressures act as a catalyst for personal growth and development or a source of stress is often the degree to which people feel they have control over how to respond. The chapter on personal resilience appears where it does in this book because managing personal energy in the ways described provides the foundation for staying in control and building personal power. Creating opportunities for people to speak freely and collaborate with others on their unique perspectives gives them a forum to use that power to move themselves and the team forward. This is much better for their wellbeing.

Small is beautiful

Many change initiatives fail because the energy that goes into envisioning the goal or 'preferred future' isn't matched by granular definition of the small sequential steps needed to get there. The complexity of the modern world means that 'normal' cause and effect chains are irrevocably disrupted, which is one of the reasons why people are so unsettled by uncertainty – and almost any change made by one person or group will have an impact somewhere else. But the process starts with an initial change and the 'disturbance' doesn't have to be big to be effective; it just has to stir the air.

Figure 5: Scaling and small steps

In our workshops, we ask teams to imagine and describe the collective 'preferred future' on any issues that they feel currently drain energy and performance. This gives them their '10' on the scaling diagram above. They're then asked to assess how far they feel they are away from that now, on a notional scale starting at 1 (as bad as that issue could possibly be) and ending at their 10 (as good as it could get). People usually say they feel they're starting somewhere between 3 and 5. In truth it doesn't really matter what the actual starting number is. What we want them to think about is what they can do, within their sphere of influence, to move them one integer up the scale *towards* 10. If you're starting at, say, 4, you don't need to worry about the details of 6, 7, 8 and beyond as you won't get that far without achieving the step from 4 to 5. It's important to visualise 10 so you feel emotionally attached and engaged with it as a goal but it's the detail of the step from 4 to 5 (or whatever is your own next step) that you'll need to focus on now.

This approach works for two reasons. The first is that small steps are more likely to be within the group's sphere of influence so they're much more likely to be realised. There's no control if you have to get someone else's budget or input to effect the change. The second is that these specific steps are shaped by the people who are directly affected by the issue needing attention – they're therefore highly invested in solving the problem. Small steps are more likely to be achievable and nothing breeds success like success. Starting out with incremental actions that can be linked, controlled and implemented but which make progress towards the direction in which they want to go not only feels better but it works better. The structured dialogue process we described earlier (Chapter 7), particularly when linked to a pre and post assessment, provides the perfect framework to facilitate the small change, big difference model.

Team vision

Discussing and agreeing preferred futures and how to make the best use of limited team energy resources inevitably stimulates discussion about important big picture areas such as team purpose, mission and values. If you get involved in a discussion of these areas in the process of agreeing the right small step actions, it often refreshes and galvanises people's commitment to shared goals. This is vital for a sense of belonging as well as good decision making about where to direct resources when they're scarce and the pressure is mounting.

Ground rules for success

The good news about ground rules is that they're simple. The whole point of the process is that whoever is facilitating, this is what they're doing – facilitating, not controlling or leading. They don't need to predict where the conversation is going – all they need to do is hold the space and let the participants generate the content. Nobody is expected to 'know' the answers, particularly if you're a manager. If you build trust, new ways of making the best use of team resources will emerge through discussion.

Trust is key here. At the beginning, people may struggle to have confidence in the process and may be slow to volunteer their opinions until it's proven to be safe to do so. Nobody will share more than they feel comfortable sharing but leaders can speed progress through this stage by showing vulnerability and sharing their own ideas and experiences, admitting they don't know how to approach a situation and thus creating a safe space for insight and knowledge sharing. People also find it easier to elucidate a problem (some like to do this in great depth) than describe what they think 'better' would look or feel like. This is where this type of regular process can come to the rescue. By creating regular, safe forums for sharing small insights and unearthing the wisdom that ripples through many different perspectives, disconnected thoughts can come together to shape solutions that people can support and feel they uncovered for themselves. The confidence to contribute to the process builds over time.

As conversations develop, everyone present should keep in mind that the first meeting is the start of the journey, not the end in itself. It's also extremely important that each team member holds themselves accountable for protecting the 'green shoots' of greater psychological safety and openness as they embark on the journey together. This means that leaders, team members or external support need to allow all voices to be heard and treat each contribution with equal respect. This is particularly important if what's offered conflicts with a personal opinion or an already established strategy. It helps to stay mindful that an opinion has no objective reality – it's the person who proffered it who lives and breathes it. Although we may not mean to, if we rubbish someone's idea or contribution we devalue them at the same time.

As covered in Chapter 7, everyone needs to assume positive intention and respond to the human behind the idea, not the idea itself. The value of insight lies in its diversity and the fresh light it throws on well-worn and familiar responses to life and work. There's little progress to be made by hearing your own voice in an echo chamber. Exploring dissonance is not only liberating for all involved, but also heavy with individual and organisational learning potential.

There will inevitably be more potential discussion topics than can be explored in a single meeting. The team should prioritise a few hot topics and stick to them. They can revisit other areas in turn in subsequent discussions. They should also aim for a balance of what's working well for them as a workgroup right now, as well as what could be improved on. It's good discipline to spend a generous amount of time actively exploring recent triumphs or little wins and looking closely at possible reasons for the successes. The likelihood is that anything that might need improvement will need to draw on those strengths or capabilities. Appreciating what these team strengths are and how they benefit is useful for both protecting these areas when the pressure's on as well as leveraging them for knotty problems or uncomfortable conversations.

Bigger circles of concern than influence

We've now outlined a simple process to release the insight capital locked up in the business and thoroughly recommend that every manager incorporates this type of activity into their leadership regularly. Doing so will be a vital and much needed first step in addressing workplace wellbeing issues by unpacking and adapting the sources of workplace pressure. This primary intervention is a vital complement to the secondary intervention of helping people develop resilience and the tertiary intervention of treatment and support when demands and challenges have gone beyond personal capacity to cope. What people have to tell you through this process will be immeasurably valuable and much of what they come up with will fall comfortably inside their circles of influence. However, people care about many more issues than they have direct influence over. To keep meetings solution focused, teams are encouraged to look for small step changes that they implement with the support of their line manager if necessary. But they will unearth systemic issues that are significantly beyond their circle of influence.

If you are to avoid the burden of fixing organisational stress problems weighing solely on the employees themselves, there obviously needs to be matching senior leadership team account-ability. Those with the appropriately larger circle of influence need to be curious about the learning potential of these types of discussions. Resources need to be devoted to willingly collecting, assimilating and acting on the issues and ideas that emerge from the process, but which employees have no capacity to implement for themselves. One of the benefits of collecting team data in a standardised way is that common themes with systemic roots can be observed quite easily. Time is at a premium everywhere and enthusiasm can wane quickly if too much digging is required. Collecting and then collating insight in this way speeds things up and makes for more focused leadership discussions.

Any leader with a bias for curiosity and who can stay open and attentive, even when the message gets uncomfortable, will be able to see patterns, common concerns and regular themes flowing from psychologically safe team dialogue. Most leaders have the skills to listen like this but a smaller number seem brave enough to take what they hear forward and do something about it. For all the reasons already covered, the focus stays (safely) on what can be done at a team level within the current guardrails. Anything falling outside that, precisely because it doesn't fit the narrative of what's possible, is often dismissed as impractical. It may even be regarded as irrelevant because the intelligence is tainted by self-interest, active disengagement or any other 'just' cause for being dismissed.

Phase 1	Phase 2	Phase 3
Assessment	Meeting Preparation	Action Planning

Phase 1 Group Report	Phase 3 SLT Review	Phase 5 Follow-up

SLT to complete the Team Energy Assessment and receive personal profiles	Anonymised SLT responses are sent to each member of the SLT	Nominated SLT member 1:1 session with internal resources to plan for SLT meeting	SLT review the group results together	SLT collectively decide which issues are most important to them and agree action points	Process is repeated to measure changes that have taken place since previous assessment

Figure 6: The senior leadership team data strand

Senior leaders can help themselves overcome this learned behaviour by creating exactly the same dedicated opportunities for open discussion described earlier, using them as a tool to unlock creative problem-solving potential in their own teams. We might assume that age and experience are linear and senior leadership are senior precisely because they have more of both. But then how much insight might be dammed up inside an echo chamber in which all senior leaders are operating on the same basis, where the way they're doing it now is the only way it can be done? What might they find out if they were to take on perspectives different to their own? What solutions might emerge if they combined their viewpoints with the insights of younger, less experienced people? Might they be deliberately involved as catalysts for such conversations about change? What if less senior people were selected for participation precisely because their lower levels of experience mean they're likely to be less entrenched in their thinking?

Such an approach might create opportunities to tackle the elephants in the room – the sources of pressure that are well outside the average employee's circle of influence but fall into their circle of concern. Ingrained systemic procedures and ways of working that all must adhere to are often a source of immense pressure, as stress surveys consistently show. All too often senior leadership pass the baton to HR, who are unable to make meaningful inroads into these issues because of their lower level of autonomy and influence. Meaning well, they bow to the pressure of immediacy, implementing the barest level of support in the hope that something is better than nothing. As a result they often leave employees feeling cynical about yet another initiative that has no significant positive impact on the pressure they feel.

Management models have evolved in recent decades. Post pandemic we see a focus on empathy, trust, resilience and growth (Bersin 2023). Such evolution now requires leaders to focus on ways to truly hear their employees, to listen and understand that, despite plucky efforts to build resilience and repair people when it all gets too much, the underlying issues generated from the top still need to be addressed. In the final analysis, not looking at the sources of workplace pressure but instead offering resilience training and counselling support is akin to cleaning up fish and throwing them back in a dirty pond.

We've shown that investing in employee wellbeing is crucial for sustainable performance. According to Deloitte's *Mental health and employers* report (2017), simply responding to your staff's mental health and wellbeing isn't enough: 'Reactive support, such as offering employees therapy or treatment once their mental health had worsened, although an important part of the suite of interventions an employer should offer, provided on average a return of only £3 for every £1 invested.' This approach essentially tackles the situation once it becomes a problem. Deloitte goes on to say, 'Organisation-wide culture change and awareness raising can provide a ROI of £6 for every £1 invested.' If ever there was a case to address those top-level organisational sources of pressure then that's it. Interestingly, Deloitte recognises that 'proactive training provides a similarly high average ROI of £5 for every £1 invested'. This indicates that organisation-wide, preventative activities to improve employee resilience can achieve a higher impact than reactive, individual-focused activities.

In addition to pleasing business leaders and CFOs, this will also be music to those HR and OH professionals who have been banging their drums for decades in an attempt to gain traction for such crucial systemic change. Additionally, COOs will heave a sigh of relief as the issues their teams have been complaining about, that make their jobs more difficult and are way beyond their scope of influence, will finally be addressed.

In our consulting, we continue to see a reluctance to get down and dirty and actually tackle those systemic issues. There are multiple reasons for this. For some, the problems simply seem too big. The perceived effort needed to open the proverbial can of worms feels too great and will detract from the day to day leadership of the organisation. The connection between addressing these issues and enhanced performance and sustainability is lost in the daily pressures of leading. Another reason is that some leaders have simply lost enthusiasm for creating change. Already fatigued by constant disruption, the appetite for change at the top level wanes, with leaders focusing instead on the issue of competi- tiveness. Again, the line of sight between addressing those top-level issues and gaining a competitive edge is lost on the weary leaders battling for pole position. Or it may be that some leaders simply don't care for anything that has a whiff of wellbeing attached to it, deeming this to be the responsibility of HR professionals (who may lack the clout required to effect change).

Whatever the reason, it's now one of the key ways to move your organisation – and keep moving it – into a positive trajectory of performance, growth and sustainability. At the same time, it will keep your top talent enthusiastic and motivated, meaning they're much more likely to remain loyal and committed to you. There's no need to shy away from such seemingly enormous elephants crowding the boardroom. The answers to your organisation's systemic sources of pressure are already there in the minds of those most affected by them. You simply need to give them the opportunity to share their insights and support them in making the necessary adjustments.

Sandboxing

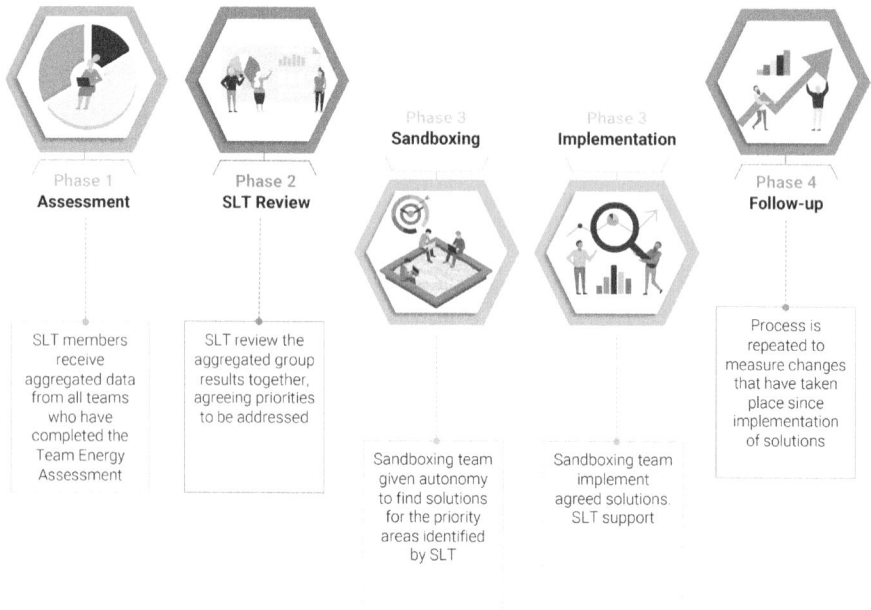

Phase 1 Assessment	Phase 2 SLT Review	Phase 3 Sandboxing	Phase 3 Implementation	Phase 4 Follow-up
SLT members receive aggregated data from all teams who have completed the Team Energy Assessment	SLT review the aggregated group results together, agreeing priorities to be addressed	Sandboxing team given autonomy to find solutions for the priority areas identified by SLT	Sandboxing team implement agreed solutions. SLT support	Process is repeated to measure changes that have taken place since implementation of solutions

Figure 7: The sandboxing strand

Nine times out of ten, the solutions to these big issues lie within your own organisation. This is where sandboxing can help (Clarke 2017). This is a simple process of the leadership cohort enabling others lower down in the organisation to tackle those systemic issues. Identifying and enabling well-connected, diversely talented individuals with the drive and energy to unpack the issues and giving them the time, budget and resources to come up with workable solutions pays dividends. Importantly, they're relieved of their day jobs, separated from their daily routine, albeit temporarily, to work on these important issues, hence the term 'sandboxing'. Finding these people is free too because, as we've said, the solutions are already in the heads of those working for you. You don't need expensive consultants to tell you what the problems are – you only need to follow a simple process that asks the right questions. You'll find the granularity you need for developing solutions from this data. Then all you need to do is trust the people in your organisation to fix them – give them the responsibility to tackle the issues. Allow them to place productivity and wellness – which is especially important given the trend towards a four-day working week – at the heart of the solutions they'll create to gain a greater sense of vocational community.

This, as you've probably realised, is a natural progression from the Team Agility type discussion covered earlier but this time aimed higher at the gnarly systemic issues that have been lurking towards the bottom of the senior leadership agenda. Create a sandboxed group of corporate intrapreneurs who can work horizontally in your organisation, who can innovate, disrupt, change the narrative and find better ways of gaining potentially even greater results (Stanford Online nd). Create a group that has a safe space (not an echo chamber) and the power, resources and capability to dig deep into the more difficult topics. This will provide you with more actionable solutions from the people that experience the issues, mined from a seam of insight that you wouldn't normally be able to reach. This is where you'll uncover the simple but profoundly beneficial changes that you could make.

Putting it all together

The two strands to focus on are, first, your own senior leadership team (SLT) data, how workplace pressures affect you and what you can do to make things easier on yourselves (Figure 6). The second strand is for your SLT cohort to take the time to safely discuss patterns in the data collected from the teams within your organisation and then to apply the sandboxing process (Figure 7). You'll find that the two strands cross over – as changes made at strand one will positively change strand two. Working on both strands together will give you a clear path towards a brave new world.

Figure 8 below illustrates how, when combined with the appropriate leadership behaviours and more psychological safety, the Team Agility style process enables two stakeholder groups to tackle local and systemic issues from their respective 'sides'. By process and data sharing in this manner they can collaborate – human to human – on improving the primary sources of poor wellbeing in the business, leveraging different perspectives to shape up the primary interventions needed to supplement resilience training and mental health support.

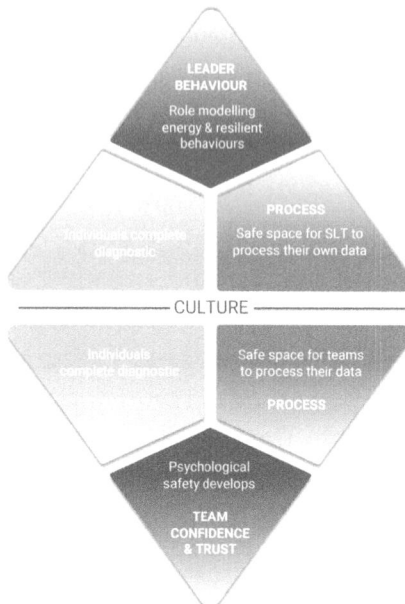

Figure 8: The intervention model

When leaders role model energy management and resilient behaviours they empower themselves to see beyond the safe and familiar, be less fearful of hearing the uncomfortable and more willing to experiment with the ideas flowing from the other, employee, side of the model. By engaging their own team in the same process, with the express purpose to challenge what they are doing and why, they release fresh insight and ideas into the mix.

Looking now at the reflected side of the model, when employees feel psychologically safe their trust and confidence in each other rapidly grows. The assessment and review process offers a safe space to use this newly acquired trust. In it they can explore fresh approaches, share insights and collaborate openly in finding solutions to joint wellbeing and performance challenges.

One size fits no one – the road ahead

Taking a more employee-centric approach to problem solving and looking for ways to meaningfully fold their unique insights into decision making at a much earlier stage is likely to be a preoccupation for senior leaders in the coming years. A new, multi-faceted workforce is emerging, one that's more diverse in age and ethnicity, is more mobile and has much stronger opinions about flexibility and work–life balance. There's no single employee proposition or wellbeing solution that will appeal to and support a workforce that's ethnically diverse and may possibly contain multiple generations.

Hybrid working has become normal within many industries and with it come unique appeals and challenges for different sectors of the team. One size does not fit everyone and may actually fit nobody at all. Managing hybrid working by mandating a set number of days per week or just hoping people will drift back into the office over time is unlikely to produce the desired result. Many workers have already demonstrated their displeasure at going back to the 'original normal' and have voted with their feet, taking jobs where they can achieve a better balance between work and the rest of life. HR management approaches that put the employee at the centre, and which demonstrate that it's the human who has been employed, not just the skillset, will be more able to attract and retain the talent they seek. It's a skill sellers' market and the transactional decision-making criteria have changed.

The westernised Generation Z cohort are no longer driven by bagging a stable job and saving up for a mortgage. With the average home deposit currently standing at £70,000, their view is often that they won't be able to get onto the property ladder, so why try? The average age at which young people leave the family home is now 25, meaning stable, full-time jobs are no longer a panacea. Many are opting instead to join the gig economy with a portfolio of jobs that offer no security but plenty of flexibility and variety. The most popular job for the under-thirties is 'social media influencer'; therefore, if you're a leader trying to attract global talent to key roles, you need to use a new model (see Channel 4 2023). Continually pushing your company's mission and purpose is unpalatable and employees today are more likely to leave and join an organisation that's serious about citizenship, learning and growth. There's even a subsection of TikTok called QuitTok, where young people post videos of themselves quitting their jobs as they rebel against relentless pressure and ever-extending working hours. Online communities such as these are a growing phenomenon.

The last word

We've spent thousands of hours in focus groups, workshops and personal support sessions hearing what employees wish their employers would allow them to change directly or what they'd like to see happen *so that they can do their jobs better or more efficiently.* As you can imagine, a small number of people would, if we let them, wax lyrical for the whole meeting about issues that, if addressed, would remove all the company's ills at a stroke. However, the incidence of soapbox issues is lower than you might imagine. What we hear instead is a great deal of small stuff – day to day irritations that rankle, deplete energy or just get in the way of doing the job people want to do. The resonant tone is one of frustration at being prevented from making the full contribution they want to make.

Underneath all the presenting issues, which are context specific to each person or team, two clear and consistent messages float up. The first is the abiding need for an employee to feel appreciated for the effort, engagement and sometimes sacrifice they offer in pursuit of company goals. The second is that employees need to feel they have some *agency*. Wrapped up in 50 different ways in every session, we hear the same message over and over again – they want to feel they have a voice, that someone is interested in what they know and that if they shared it, even if it wasn't acted on, their input would be seen as valuable.

The people we meet in focus groups and workshops are just like you. The people you have responsibility for if you're a manager, or just collaborate with if you're not, are also just like them. There are literally hundreds of voices out there waiting to be heard and willing to share their learning with you, for free. If you sit down now and read management books for the rest of the year, what you read between the pages is unlikely to be more valuable to you *right now* than the information and insight your colleagues are walking about with in their heads. So, starting today, if you're a leader, make it your mission to make it safe for your team to use their voices and tell you what they know. Whether you're a leader or not, be authentic and brave about sharing your insight when you can see a better way forward.

In our turbulent times, there's white water everywhere but people don't have to fall out of the boat on the way down the company rapids. Let's all agree to speak up, be more curious about knowledge and perspectives that diverge from our own, keep everyone in the boat *and* enjoy the thrill of the ride!

Chapter 8: Big questions

- ★ If you're a **team member**: how can you expand your circle of influence? What can you get involved in right now that will help address some of the issues you're facing?
- ★ If you're a **people leader**: when will you organise a meeting for your team to discuss the sources of pressure they're under and how it's affecting them? Can you give them the authority to make small changes at a local level to relieve the pressure and make their working lives less pressured and more productive?
- ★ If you're a **senior leader**: when will you discuss at your level how pressure impacts you and your peers? How will you address these issues? Importantly, when will you create a group of corporate intrapreneurs to tackle the big issues running through your organisation?

Key messages

- ★ The world of work is changing and leaders need to get on board and rethink their management model in order to tempt global talent to their organisations.
- ★ Be brave and find out what the issues are in your organisation. Gather data and act upon it at all levels, including your own.
- ★ Most solutions lie inside your organisation. Trust your people to find the right solutions and give them the resources from which to do so.

Acknowledgements

During our nearly three decades of consulting, we have been fortunate to work alongside some of the most inspirational minds in the industry, among them Professor Cary Cooper CBE, Dr Richard Heron, Dr Martyn Davidson, Clare Walsh, Paul Schofield, Dr Ian Wright, Sue Cruse, Dr Anne Finn, Dr Sarah Forsythe, Marcus Hunt, Jay Brewer, Dr Robert Willcox, Dr Noel McElearney, Dr Doreen Miller, Gary Billotti, Sylvia Rohde-Liebenau, Dr Les Smith and many other pioneers of proactive and sources-based employee wellbeing management. We have been privileged to work alongside you and we are indebted to you all.

Special mention also for Elizabeth Gyngell, now retired from the UK Health and Safety Executive, who championed management standards based on the benefits of formal psychosocial risk assessment and involving employees directly in risk moderation. This 'led from the top – fed from the bottom' approach remains central to our consulting model today and, as we move towards ever more diverse workforces, has more resonance now than ever.

Our unbridled gratitude also to the founder of our original consulting business, the late Dr Stephen Williams, and for his productive partnership with our late systems developer Martyn Sandbrook. Between them they found a way to combine investigative and academic rigour with rapidity, and in so doing make the process of identifying 'how good the work is' possible. We miss them both more than words can say.

Huge thanks to Liza Hutton, for being the most amazingly thoughtful and supportive friend and colleague and whose patience and ability to derive meaning and intention from the most inadequate or rambling briefing is legendary. Thank you for all that you have personally contributed to this book, not just through its many revisions, platform alterations and redesigns, but for always being a listening ear for the frustrations of writing, as well as the out-loud rehearsal of half-formed thoughts, usually when you are busy doing something else. Thank you also for all the midnight oil burnt getting each of the models and images into the right shape for publication – particularly the ones that came to you as scribbled drawings in the middle of the night. Our gratitude and admiration for you knows no bounds.

Our generous thanks to the whole team at The Right Book Company, particularly our editors Beverley Glick and Andrew Chapman and Paul East our production supremo. Everyone involved has been endlessly supportive and unfailingly patient during changes of intellectual direction, resultant manuscript delays and all the associated agonies of book design. Sue Richardson, you have a great team!

Finally, but by no means least, our joint love and thanks to our separate but several long-suffering partners, family members and friends, all of whom were regularly inconvenienced by looming (feared to be missed) internal and external writing deadlines. Thank you for your patience and gentle recognition that the writing path is rutted and that yet again you will have to get a take-out!

We would also both like to apologise to our dogs for all the walks that did not, in the end, materialise – we will make it up to you!

Lesley Cooper & Vicky Smith

Resources

Chapter 1

Harvard Business School (2020) 'Collaborating during coronavirus: the impact of COVID-19 on the nature of work', Harvard Business School Organisational Behavior Unit/Strategy Unit Working Paper No 21-006. URL: papers.ssrn.com/sol3/papers.cfm?abstract_id=3654470

Waddell, G & Burton, A K (2006) 'Is work good for your health and well-being?' URL: assets.publishing.service.gov.uk/government/uploads/system/uploads/attachment_data/file/209510/hwwb-is-work-good-for-you-exec-summ.pdf

Lipman, J (2021) 'The pandemic revealed how much we hate our jobs. Now we have a chance to reinvent work'. TIME, 27 May. URL: time.com/6051955/work-after-covid-19

Storr, W (2019) *The Science of Storytelling: Why stories make us human, and how to tell them better*. William Collins.

Frankl, V E (1985) 'The will to meaning', from *Man's Search for Meaning*. Simon & Schuster. URL: panarchy.org/frankl/meaning.html

Sinek, S (2009) *Start with Why*. Penguin Business.

Coyle, D (2018) *The Culture Code*. Random House Business.

Health & Safety Executive (2022) 'Work-related stress, anxiety or depression statistics in Great Britain, 2022'. URL: hse.gov.uk/statistics/causdis/stress.pdf

McKinsey & Company (2022) 'Gone for now, or gone for good? How to play the new talent game and win back workers'. URL: mckinsey.com/capabilities/people-and-organizational-performance/our-insights/gone-for-now-or-gone-for-good-how-to-play-the-new-talent-game-and-win-back-workers

Steiner S, Cropley M et al (2020) 'Reasons for staying with your employer: Identifying the key organizational predictors of employee retention within a global energy business'. *Journal of Occupational and Environmental Medicine* 62(4).

Chapter 2

Stone, L (2009) 'Beyond simple multi-tasking: continuous partial attention'. URL: lindastone.net/2009/11/30/beyond-simple-multi-tasking-continuous-partial-attention

Dreher, D E (2018) 'Too much to do in too little time?', *Psychology Today*. URL: psychologytoday.com/gb/blog/your-personal-renaissance/201803/too-much-do-in-too-little-time

Schwartz, T, Gomes, J & McCarthy C (2010) *The Way We're Working Isn't Working*. Simon & Schuster.

JInsider (2009) 'Rabbi Dr Abraham Twerski on responding to stress'. URL: youtube.com/watch?v=3aDXM5H-Fuw

Wikipedia (2004) 'Yerkes–Dodson law'. URL: en.wikipedia.org/wiki/Yerkes–Dodson_law

Gould, D, & Krane, V (1992) 'The arousal–athletic performance relationship: Current status and future directions'. In T. S. Horn (ed.), *Advances in sport psychology*. Human Kinetics Publishers.

Sinek, S (2019) 'Trusting teams: the 5 practices'. URL: youtube.com/watch?v=W5qQJhe7sLE

Edmondson, A C (2018) *The Fearless Organisation*. Harvard Business School/Wiley.

Chapter 3

Kubler-Ross, E (1969) *On Death and Dying*. Macmillan.

Endocrine Society (2022) 'Brain hormones'. URL: endocrine.org/patient-engagement/endocrine-library/hormones-and-endocrine-function/brain-hormones

World Health Organization (2022) 'World mental health report: transforming mental health for all'. URL: who.int/publications/i/item/9789240049338

Bonde J P E (2008) 'Psychosocial factors at work and risk of depression: a systematic review of the epidemiological evidence'. *Occupational and Environmental* 65.

HSE (2022) 'Work-related stress, anxiety or depression statistics in Great Britain, 2022'. URL: hse.gov.uk/statistics/causdis/stress.pdf

Whitehouse, J, Micheletta, J & Waller, B M (2017) 'Stress behaviours buffer macaques from aggression'. *Scientific Reports* 7, 11083.

Sabel, B A, Wang, J, et al (2018). 'Mental stress as consequence and cause of vision loss: the dawn of psychosomatic ophthalmology for preventive and personalized medicine'. *EPMA Journal* 9(2).

ScienceDaily (2009) 'Stress puts double whammy on reproductive system, fertility'. URL: sciencedaily.com/releases/2009/06/090615171618.htm

Tennant, C (2000) 'Work stress and coronary heart disease'. *Journal of Cardiovascular Risk* 7(4).

Pandya, D (1998) 'Psychological stress, emotional behavior and coronary heart disease'. *Comprehensive Therapy* 24(5).

Hassoun, L, Herrmann-Lingen, C et al (2015) 'Association between chronic stress and blood pressure: findings from the German Health Interview and Examination Survey for Adults 2008–2011'. *Psychosomatic Medicine* 77(5).

Morey, J N, Boggero, I A et al (2015) 'Current directions in stress and human immune function'. *Current Opinion in Psychology* Oct 1 5.

Fortunato, V J & Harsh, J (2006). 'Stress and sleep quality: the moderating role of negative affectivity'. *Personality and Individual Differences* 41(5).

Kucharczyk, E R, Morgan, K & Hall, A P (2012) 'The occupational impact of sleep quality and insomnia symptoms'. *Sleep Medicine Reviews* 16(6).

Salvagioni D A J, Melanda F N et al (2017) 'Physical, psychological and occupational consequences of job burnout: a systematic review of prospective studies'. *PLoS ONE* 12(1).

Fletcher, B C (1988) 'Occupation, marriage and disease-specific mortality'. *Social Science and Medicine* 77.

DWP/DHSC (2017) 'Thriving at work: the Stevenson/Farmer review of mental health and employers'. URL: assets.publishing.service.gov.uk/government/uploads/system/uploads/attachment_data/file/658145/thriving-at-work-stevenson-farmer-review.pdf

Deloitte (2022) 'Poor mental health costs UK employers up to £56 billion a year'. URL: www2.deloitte.com/uk/en/pages/press-releases/articles/poor-mental-health-costs-uk-employers-up-to-pound-56-billion-a-year.html

Little, B & Little, P (2006) 'Employee engagement: conceptual issues'.

Journal of Organisational Culture, Communications and Conflict 10(1).

HRreview (2014) 'It costs over £30K to replace a staff member'. URL: hrreview.co.uk/hr-news/recruitment/it-costs-over-30k-to-replace-a-staff-member/50677

Chapter 4

Evans-Lacko, S, Corker, E et al (2014) 'Effect of the Time to Change anti-stigma campaign on trends in mental-illness-related public stigma among the English population in 2003–13: an analysis of survey data'. *The Lancet Psychiatry* 1(2).

Javed, M. (2020) *Stress Management Industry: Global Trends*. BCC Research.

Callaghan, S, Lösch, M et al (2021) 'Feeling good: the future of the $1.5 trillion wellness market'. URL: https://www.mckinsey.com/industries/consumer-packaged-goods/our-insights/feeling-good-the-future-of-the-1-5-trillion-wellness-market

Covey, S R (nd) 'Big rocks'. URL: resources.franklincovey.com/the-8th-habit/big-rocks-stephen-r-covey

Waddell, G & Burton, A K (2006) – see Chapter 1 references.

Chapter 5

Schein, E H & Bennis, W G (1965) *Personal and Organizational Change through Group Methods: The laboratory approach*. Wiley.

Edmondson A C (2019) *The Fearless Organisation: Creating psychological safety in the workplace for learning, innovation, and growth*. Wiley.

Altman, D (nd) 'What is psychological safety at work? How leaders can build psychologically safe workplaces'. URL: ccl.org/articles/leading-effectively-articles/what-is-psychological-safety-at-work

Duhigg, C (2016) 'What Google learned from its quest to build the perfect team'. *New York Times Magazine*. URL: nytimes.com/2016/02/28/magazine/what-google-learned-from-its-quest-to-build-the-perfect-team.html

Edmondson A C (1996) 'Learning from mistakes is easier said than done: Group and organizational influences on the detection and correction of human error'. *Journal of Applied Behavioral Science* 32(1).

Peters, S (2013) *The Chimp Paradox: The mind management program to help you achieve success, confidence, and happiness.* Tarcher-Perigee.

Luft, J & Ingham, H (1955) 'The Johari window, a graphic model of interpersonal awareness'. *Proceedings of the Western Training Laboratory in Group Development,* University of California.

Guest, D (1991) 'The hunt is on for the Renaissance Man of computing'. *The Independent* 17/9/91.

Dilts, R, Hallbom, T & Smith, S (2012) *Beliefs: Pathways to health and well-being.* Crown House Publishing.

Somogyi, R L, Buchko, A A & Buchko, K J (2013) 'Managing with empathy: can you feel what I feel?' *Journal of Organizational Psychology* 13(1/2).

Meechan, F, McCann, L & Cooper, C (2022) 'The importance of empathy and compassion in organizations: why there is so little, and why we need more'. In *Research Handbook on the Sociology of Organizations.* Edward Elgar Publishing.

Chabrak, N, Craig, R & Daidj, N (2016) 'Financialization and the employee suicide crisis at France Telecom'. *Journal of Business Ethics* 139(3).

Callahan, S (2018) 'Putting stories to work: Discover'. *Knowledge Management Matters, 51*.

Gratton, L & Erickson, T J (2007) 'Eight ways to build collaborative teams'. *Harvard Business Review* November 2007. URL: hbr.org/2007/11/eight-ways-to-build-collaborative-teams

Chapter 6

Loehr, J & Schwartz, T (2006) *The Power of Full Engagement: Managing energy, not time, is the key to high performance and personal renewal.* Gabler.

George, B (2010) *True North: Discover your authentic leadership.* Wiley.

Frankl, V (1985) – see Chapter 1 references.

Schwartz, T & McCarthy, C (2007) 'Manage your energy, not your time'. *Harvard Business Review* 85(10).

Mulford, P (1889) *Prentice Mulford's Story: Life by land and sea.* FJ Needham.

Petruzzello, S J, Han, M & Nowell, P (1997) 'The influence of physical fitness and exercise upon cognitive functioning: a meta-analysis'. *Journal of Sport and Exercise Psychology* 19.

Karpman, S B (2019) 'Don't say anything you can't diagram: the creative brainstorming system of Eric Berne'. *International Journal of Transactional Analysis Research and Practice* 10(1).

Freedman, J (2007) 'The physics of emotion: Candace Pert on feeling Go(o)d'. URL: 6seconds.org/2007/01/26/the-physics-of-emotion-candace-pert-on-feeling-good

Cleveland Clinic (2022) 'Serotonin'. URL: my.clevelandclinic.org/health/articles/22572-serotonin

ScienceDirect (2023) 'Monamine neurotransmitter'. URL: sciencedirect.com/topics/neuroscience/monoamine-neurotransmitter

Simons, I (2009) 'Why do we have emotions?'. URL: psychologytoday.com/us/blog/the-literary-mind/200911/why-do-we-have-emotions

Thorsen, S V, Pedersen, J et al (2019) 'Perceived stress and sickness absence: a prospective study of 17,795 employees in Denmark'. *International Archives of Occupational and Environmental Health* 92.

McEwen B S (1998) 'Stress, adaptation, and disease: allostasis and allostatic load'. *Annals of the New York Academy of Sciences* 840.

Schwartz et al (2010) – see Chapter 2 references.

Gerasimo, P (2020) 'Use the science of ultradian rhythms to boost productivity, energy, and willpower'. URL: bluezones.com/2020/06/how-taking-breaks-can-increase-productivity-boost-energy-levels-and-help-you-show-up-in-your-life/

Franscisco (2017) 'Difference between capability and competency'. URL: differencebetween.net/language/words-language/difference-between-capability-and-competency

Stone, L (nd) 'FAQ'. URL: lindastone.net/faq

Pruyn, P (2018) 'Continuous partial attention and the demise of discretionary time'. URL: thesystemsthinker.com/continuous-partial-attention-and-the-demise-of-discretionary-time/

Fox, A (1996) 'Reflex and reflectivity: Wuwei in the Zhuangzi'. *Asian Philosophy* 6(1).

Chapter 7

Jeffers, S (2012) *Feel the Fear and Do It Anyway*. Random House.

Velasquez, M, Andre, C et al (1988) 'Ethics and virtue'. *Issues in Ethics* 1(3).

Schwartz, J, Eaton, K et al (2021) 'The worker-employer relationship disrupted'. URL: www2.deloitte.com/us/en/insights/focus/human-capital-trends/2021/the-evolving-employer-employee-relationship.html

Goffee, R & Jones, G (2013) 'Creating the best workplace on Earth'. *Harvard Business Review* May 2013. URL: hbr.org/2013/05/creating-the-best-workplace-on-earth

Chapter 8

Bersin, J (2023) 'HR predictions for 2023'. URL: jbc.joshbersin.com/wp-content/uploads/2023/01/WT-23_01-HR-Predictions-2023-Report.pdf

Deloitte (2017) 'Mental health and employers: refreshing the case for investment'. URL: www2.deloitte.com/uk/en/pages/consulting/articles/mental-health-and-employers-refreshing-the-case-for-investment.html

Clarke, D (2017) 'The serious business of sandboxes'. URL: strategy-business.com/article/The-Serious-Business-of-Sandboxes

Stanford Online (nd) 'What is intrapreneurship, and how can you cultivate it at your company?'. URL: online.stanford.edu/what-intrapreneurship-and-how-can-you-cultivate-it-your-company

Channel 4 (2023) *Kathy Burke: Growing up*. URL: channel4.com/programmes/kathy-burke-growing-up

About the authors

Vicky Smith

Vicky is a true change agent who has more than 20 years' experience of consulting, coaching, facilitation and training in locations across the globe. She holds an MSc in Organisation Development and Consultancy, an MSc in Psychology and an MSc in Applied Health and Exercise. She is currently halfway through a PhD, researching psychological safety in organisations, and is also a qualified NLP trainer, psychotherapist and executive coach.

She began her consulting career in 1994 as an Investors in People advisor and assessor and left corporate employment having reached senior status with responsibility for the strategic development needs of an organisation employing more than 35,000 people. Her enthusiasm for what she does energises and motivates those around her and generates drive and accountability.

A lifelong learner, Vicky is passionate about sharing her knowledge and experience with others in a pragmatic way, helping others achieve their goals and step into the best versions of themselves. She lives in the south-east of England with her family and menagerie of animals and has a passion for the Scottish Highlands, canicross (cross-country running with dogs) and the creative arts.

Lesley Cooper

Lesley is the founder of WorkingWell Ltd, a specialist health and performance consultancy based in London, whose focus is the proactive and cost-effective management of employee wellbeing and performance.

She has more than 25 years' experience in the design and delivery of all elements of employee wellbeing and performance strategy, with particular interest in psychosocial risk management, specifically unpacking the variables at play in the dynamic relationship between workplace pressure and employee performance.

She regularly speaks about occupational stress, team and personal resilience, energy management and the active use of pressure and recovery as a catalyst for sustainable high performance both in the UK and abroad. She is co-author with the late Dr Stephen Williams of *Dangerous Waters – Strategies for Improving Wellbeing at Work*, published by John Wiley & Sons in 1999, and *Managing Workplace Stress – a best practice blueprint*, published by CBI Books in 2002. She has also contributed to several TV and radio programmes about employee wellbeing, including Channel 4's highly acclaimed documentary *Stressed Out*. She is also a full member of the International Stress Management Association. Lesley lives in Surrey with her husband, three grown-up children, four horses and the family dog.

About WorkingWell

WorkingWell is a specialist management consultancy that offers the guidance, tools and support that many companies, both large and small, are finding they need to sustain healthy, high-performance workforces.

Founded by Lesley in 1997, when UK companies and government were exploring more proactive responses to employee sickness absence than simply counting the cost of it, our service offering has expanded in line with the rapid growth of interest in employee wellbeing and the link to company performance. Originally focused around achieving more granular measurement of important employee wellbeing risk factors, specifically the sources and behavioural moderators of workplace stress, the business now consults on all aspects of employee wellbeing management.

Measurement and ensuring better targeting of existing interventions remains foundational to much of our work, however, with Vicky joining the team in 2012, having a background in organisation, people development, health science and psychology. A typical week might also see us consulting on wellbeing strategy creation and engagement, delivering scalable programmes to build personal and team energy, resilience and affiliation, as well as supporting leaders and managers in releasing discretionary effort within their teams, ensuring both wellbeing and sustainable high performance are attained. While this is going on, other members of the team may also be providing onsite or virtual emotional health support to employees and managers or engaged in 1:1 wellbeing or performance coaching at any and all levels of seniority.

How well are your teams, and how well are they working?

Feel free to contact us at team@workingwell.co.uk for a no-obligation consultation. We can help you get the most from the wellbeing investment you are already making, as well as guide you to the tools and approaches that will enable you to move more rapidly and effectively along your own 'road of most resistance'. Wherever you are on your personal or corporate wellbeing journey, we are confident we can get you there faster and in better shape!